AUDREY JEANETTE PRISK

All The Men I've Ever Dated (And Other Ghost Stories)

An honest collection of anecdotes inspired by grace, growing, and the belief that dating can be intentional.

First published by Self-Published 2021

Copyright © 2021 by Audrey Jeanette Prisk

All rights reserved. No part of this publication may be reproduced, stored or transmitted in any form or by any means, electronic, mechanical, photocopying, recording, scanning, or otherwise without written permission from the publisher. It is illegal to copy this book, post it to a website, or distribute it by any other means without permission.

Audrey Jeanette Prisk asserts the moral right to be identified as the author of this work.

Audrey Jeanette Prisk has no responsibility for the persistence or accuracy of URLs for external or third-party Internet Websites referred to in this publication and does not guarantee that any content on such Websites is, or will remain, accurate or appropriate.

Designations used by companies to distinguish their products are often claimed as trademarks. All brand names and product names used in this book and on its cover are trade names, service marks, trademarks and registered trademarks of their respective owners. The publishers and the book are not associated with any product or vendor mentioned in this book. None of the companies referenced within the book have endorsed the book.

Some names and identifying details have been changed to protect the privacy of individuals. All written content is the opinion of the author and does not reflect the opinion of any other entity mentioned in this book.

Book photography by Sadie Schwanberg

First edition

ISBN: 9798597106427

This book was professionally typeset on Reedsy.
Find out more at reedsy.com

I would like to acknowledge my sister, Anne, who has walked me through every one of these seasons of life. Sometimes, she was cheering me on from the sidelines and sometimes, she was literally spoon feeding me, but she's always been there.

My parents: wrapped up in this book is all my love for you, regardless of how much I complain about your strict rules and all the boys you scared away. I am forever grateful for your love and support.

To all who have read and encouraged, thank you.

Contents

	Foreword	ii
	Preface	iii
1	Chapter 1: Firsts	1
2	Chapter 2: It's Not You, It's My Expectations	18
3	Chapter 3: Vulnerability	25
4	Chapter 4: Worthiness	32
5	Chapter 5: High School	40
6	Chapter 6: Modern Dating and Special-Order Fiancés	44
7	Chapter 7: Truth	52
8	Chapter 8: Inner Revelation	57
9	Chapter 9: Tell It Like It Is and More Forgiveness	63
10	Chapter 10: Healing	67
11	Chapter 11: The End	77

Foreword

I started writing this book back in 2014. As the life I was living unfolded behind me, I wrote out the pieces of it all and began stringing them together like pearls on a 1920's necklace. Every story is written from my perspective and my experience. Each name has been changed, each character, while taken from my own life, has been rewritten in a way to protect the individual privacy of the beautiful people in this book who have, in their own ways, taught me what it means to be a whole, responsible, loving person. While this book is a memoir written to reflect my own personal recollections, my heart and intent is to express gratitude to those I have met along the way who have in turn, guided me here. Dialogue has been re-written for the same reason, although the intention has been left unaltered. It has been a process of looking back with respect for those who have uncovered my own notions about love and I'm grateful to each and every one of them.

I'm ready to move forward and to let these pages serve as my stake in the ground for a season of life I've passed through. The truth is, all of it means nothing if we don't stay teachable. The saddest thing anyone has ever said to me is, "I'm too old to change." So, if any of what you find here speaks to you, don't be afraid to implement it. Don't be afraid to share it with others, for it is through sharing that I have come to know my truest self.

Preface

Have you ever had your dreams run out on you? Have you ever been led into a vision of your future, only to get hit by the new reality that you have to start from scratch? This is the thing we live our lives hoping to never have to go through. This is the thing we avoid at all costs.

But I hope you get the chance to go through it. I hope that, one day, you have to decide all over again what you want to be when you grow up. I hope you come up with an amazing idea for your life only to have to re-design it into something better than you could have imagined the first time. I hope that you get the opportunity to watch your true friends rise to your heartbreak and surround you, and I hope that you don't hold back this time.

I didn't use to believe all that. I used to believe that the original plans I made for my life were good enough. I used to tiptoe around what I wanted and call it my future, and I am so thankful for the chance to make my rough draft a final edit, having been proofread by the most creative and life-giving author of all time.

Somehow, when I was a child, I adopted the thought that there was a "perfect" way to do life. I thought that there needed to be a "right way" to do everything; from getting straight As, to going to college, getting married, and everything in between. I had wrapped myself tightly in what I thought were the shoulds and should nots of life while holding myself to an impossibly high standard and only celebrating when that standard was reached. The concept of grace wasn't introduced into my life until I was 23 years old. Up until that point, I'd heard about it and talked about it, but only from a very shallow place. It was only once I found myself in the place of desperately needing grace did I realize its true nature.

The funny thing is, grace is not elusive. It stands in front of us and asks to be picked up, like the reaching arms of a young child needing comfort and acceptance. But if we never look down, we don't see it. If we never step before grace and reach back for it, we don't get to experience it. The thing we need to most understand in this life gives itself away freely to our "yes," - it stays vulnerable in front of us, asking to be picked up until we decide we're ready for it. And then, it changes our lives completely.

Admittedly harder to pinpoint than other ideas, grace is that sigh of relief when you realize you don't have to pretend anymore. Grace is the wave of acceptance that comes when the truth that you offer more than enough without accolades or opinions washes over you; when you realize you're worthy of love and acceptance just as you are. Grace is your authentic self free from comparison. Grace is the ability to recognize what you are deserving of without having to perform for it or prove yourself. Grace is that step forward into freedom and joy that comes when you embrace your true identity. And, as if that isn't amazing enough, grace has a best friend: forgiveness. They stand together, elbows linked, singing and swaying and giggling in the face of pride and denial, ready to sweep us off our feet and heal every wound, raising us up to a foundation of truth.

For me, discovering grace occurred in a moment of relationship ruin. I found myself in a place I never wanted to be, and I needed grace to get through it. Later on, I needed forgiveness to mend the ruins. Relationships, and I mean the romantic kind, have always been difficult for me to navigate, but I wasn't able to see why until my mid-twenties – until the relationship I'd hoped for from day one turned out to be something vastly different from what my expectations had grown me into believing.

I've come to learn that the biggest misconception we could ever have about life is to believe that the point is to have it all figured out before we go through it, or even while we go through it. Each day is a new opportunity to make conscious choices and take full ownership of them. This series of choices leads us to create our life, and, contrary to a worldly opinion, life is not hiding itself from us waiting for us to figure it out. We make it as we go, mostly fooling ourselves into thinking we have any kind of greater control than our own moment-to-moment choices. Are we going to choose to be a present individual with a valuable say in the decision process, or are we going to go along for the ride, wondering when it is we plateau at the horizon line of our future, only to realize it doesn't look how we expected? Are we going to skim over the pain of whatever last hurt us and numb it with fillers, or are we going to dive into the depths of vulnerability, forgiveness, and grace in order to come out a stronger person, capable of experiencing true joy and lasting freedom? Are we going to respond quietly or boisterously, and with disgust or approval? With honesty or lies? With humility or pride? With love? With forgiveness? With grace?

To live the vibrant lives we were put on this earth to live, we have to go to the depths. We have to explore the full spectrum of these difficult ideas in order to treat people with the full worth they were intentionally designed with. From the perspective of a single woman approaching 30, dating and relationships are massively lacking these things in my generation, so that is where this book is going; from the hilarity of childhood crushes to the big heartaches of adulthood, and everything that happens in between.

There's no chapter on dating well in the bible. There are, however, hundreds of examples of how to treat others as worthless (polygamy, incest, adultery, you name it, it's there) but there are also countless ways that we glimpse the beauty that is intended for our relationships. We can read about the vision God has for relationships and how to get there in a healthy way that makes families stronger and brings freedom to everyone experiencing the relationship. Before you throw up the 'ifs' and 'buts,' let me say that I know full well that not everyone was meant to be or longs to be married. We are, however, meant to love one another well, with all the fullness of love and grace that our creator has offered us. Regardless of the kinds of relationships in your life and the journey you are on, the nature and necessity of grace and forgiveness do not change.

1

Chapter 1: Firsts

I was nineteen years old when I had my first kiss. Ironically, it was twelve years earlier in first grade when I received my first marriage proposal and almost went through with a wildly spontaneous wedding under the shade of a large Oak tree on our elementary school playground. It was at that moment I began wondering what the big deal about relationships was.

It was sixth grade when I stuffed myself in a locker to avoid being asked out by a boy I couldn't actually stand. Back in that day, we called it "going out." Not sure what the kids are saying nowadays, but, "will you go out with me" was the phrase every sixth grade girl wanted to hear from her crush. No one ever thought to ask where it was they wanted to go, it was strictly a yes or no question, which looking back, made absolutely no sense.

I was asked out a lot in grade school, mostly due to the fact that for five back-to-back years, I was the curiosity striking "new girl" who had become a rather colorful social butterfly due to attending a succession of different elementary schools from Kindergarten to fourth grade. I also had the heart of an emotionally gushing fire hydrant who didn't know how to stand up for herself - an issue which has since been straightened out thanks to early encouragement from my older sister.

I remember the series of events in sixth grade the day the aforementioned locker-stuffing incident occurred. A kid I had barely had any interaction with came sprinting down the hallway to where my undersized frame stood grabbing books out of my backpack.

"Paul is coming to ask you out," he slid out through a sixth grader smirk. This messenger was the king of sixth grade. He was popular, had parents who let him eat the delicious kind of cereal, and he always seemed to know everyone's business. I froze in fear as he spun on the heels of his Chuck Taylors and sauntered back down the hallway. And then I heard them: the confident sound of worn sneakers hitting the large squares of pink-flecked tile that lined our school's hallway. Paul was approaching.

As he rounded the corner, I did the only thing a pint-sized 12-year-old could do when their school locker had previously belonged to a student three times their size. I stepped inside and closed the door behind me. Clutching my books to my chest, I peered through the metal slits into the hallway. Paul had paused, unsure of what move to make next. And then, he did the worst thing. He walked right up to my locker, stuck his mouth in front of those metal slits, and said,

"Audrey, I know you're in there. I want to ask you a question." I said nothing.

"Audrey, seriously? I know you're there."

"Go away, Paul." I broke my silence and called it brave.

"Okay, but you're being ridiculous." He stood there, expecting maturity. Expecting me to unlock my locker and step out to face him. I did none of the above.

"Go to class." I scolded him, late to class myself.

Reluctantly, Paul turned and walked back down the hallway to homeroom. I flipped the metal latch from the inside and stumbled out into the fresh air and freedom... but it didn't matter. By the time I arrived

CHAPTER 1: FIRSTS

late into homeroom, everyone knew what had happened because the sixth grade king had held down his reign by spreading the news like wildfire. Even though Paul never actually got the opportunity to ask me out, everyone already thought that the worst had happened. I grew increasingly embarrassed and slid down in my seat, determined to make it through the rest of the day without anyone else giggling their way through the letters in my name.

That afternoon and every afternoon, Paul and I rode the same hot and sticky polyester bus seats home from school. If you lived on the west side of town, you got on the bus that took you to West High School, where you then got on another bus that took you home. If you lived on the east side, you had a bus that went the other way. While the sixth grade king clunked up the stairs of the east side bus, I continued to simmer under a cloud of embarrassment from the morning's excitement as I made my way up the steps of the bus for students heading west.

As per usual, Paul was being loud in the back of the yellow metal kid chauffeur, and this is where my memory gets a little hazy because I'd already started to see red back in homeroom. He called out to me in a teasing way and I'd had it. I stood to my feet like a soldier at attention, whipped around to face him, and in a voice loud enough for the rest of the back half of the bus to hear, said a phrase I'd heard a junior high schooler say once that is demeaning enough to make the receiver deeply embarrassed and mean enough to make them stop talking altogether. Only now that I actually know what said phrase means do I realize just how awful my repeating it was. But in defense of my sixth grade self, I had no idea what I was actually saying.

This phrase was lousy enough for Paul to respond with bright red cheeks and 20 seconds of hanging his head in silence, but this is a sixth grade boy we're talking about. While Paul left me alone for the rest of the bus ride and never tried to ask me out again, he continued his rollicking the whole way to West High School. Which was fine with me, because I considered the day an overall victory.

Now that I'm older and have gone through various degrees of unpacking my responses to tense situations, also known as fight or flight, I can see the issue is not that Paul had a crush on me; that's a perfectly normal thing for that age and time of life. The issue with this moment in time is that my aversion to potentially being considered someone's girlfriend caused me to respond to the other party with resentment, almost pure hatred. I had developed a "how dare you" attitude towards anyone who thought they had the freedom to ask me to be their girlfriend. I was further offended by the fact that I had no feelings for this person, a detail I felt like they totally disregarded in their pursuit of my "yes." But whose responsibility is it to inform of feelings or not, and when? The only way to find out if your romantic notions towards another person are mutual is to pursue them, but something about that has never sat with me well.

A theme I picked up on from the few tv shows I watched while growing up and plethora of Disney movies is that only when a girl found out that a boy had feelings for her did she grow flattered and entertain the idea of dating him. The fact that she never had feelings for this person before this point never seemed to come up. Now that I'm older and recognize this as concerning, I can pick apart our desire as women to be admired and pursued. As young females, we've been shown culturally that it is our womanly duty to feel flattered when someone tells us that they think we are attractive, validating in some strange way that we are worth pursuing. The truth is, the knowledge of this attraction should have no pull over our own feelings; as if someone else's affections for us is a rare opportunity that we must pounce at when it becomes known and available to us. We have the full ability to make our own romantic decisions regardless of someone else's feelings toward us. We also have the full knowledge that attraction is objective even though our culture has done an excellent job at perpetuating the idea of beauty being measurable.

I think the root of this issue is truly learning our real identity and

CHAPTER 1: FIRSTS

knowing that our full worth is not determined or even influenced by someone else's thoughts or opinions of us. But for some reason, when the possibility of love is involved, we tend to throw this truth out the window and fill up on another's affirmations of our worthiness instead of our own. Until the real, ultimate truth of our worth provides us with an unshakeable foundation, we run the risk of requiring validation from others to feel worthy and wanted.

I clearly mistook Paul's feelings for validation. I couldn't handle even the smallest association to someone else's feelings of attraction, to the point that I hid myself away. It took years for me to learn that honoring another person meant responding to their vulnerability with truth of my own, even if it meant telling them, actually communicating to them, that my feelings didn't match theirs.

When I was in fourth grade, I used to get home about an hour before the rest of my family. I would use this precious alone time to do something I technically wasn't allowed to do: watch *Xena: Warrior Princess*. I say I technically wasn't allowed to do this because my parents never said, "you're not allowed to watch *Xena: Warrior Princess*," but that's because they didn't know I was watching *Xena: Warrior Princess*. But if they had known, they most certainly would have said not to do it. My mom would skip over select Ricky Martin songs on the one album of his we owned to keep us from hearing phrases like, "I feel a mad connection to your body." So yeah, this tv show definitely would not have worked on the appropriateness scale.

But for the short time in which the show aired on daytime TV, I would prop my backpack carelessly up against our ivory living room couch and practice poor posture in the face of Lucy Lawless and Renee O'Connor's many adventures, imagining I was there with them waving around a sword and calling out with my own warrior cry.

Out of all my days of watching this show, the one episode that replays in my memory is easily accessible for the reasons that it's slightly graphic, but also simultaneously empowering. In episode 124, Caligula, a man known to be an immortal, has beef with Xena. Xena gets close enough to kiss him, only to bite his lip and make him bleed. He pulls back in shock and touches the bright red blood dripping from his bottom lip that he can't believe is real. Xena smiles because she knows he holds no power over her (she made an immortal bleed, for crying out loud) and because she's shown him that he's been operating out of a false sense of control over her and other people.

There are many other details to this episode, some that for the sake of decency will be left out, but that's how my adolescent brain interpreted the events of those 45 minutes. I realized that even though later on in the episode, Xena loses her physical ability to kill this horrible woman-using immortal, she retains the power to convince him of the fact that his life is not more important than the lives of others. Her ability to recognize that her identity never coexisted with this man's ability to overpower her physically or emotionally stayed with me forever. I looked up to the fact that even though she knew that he had power, she did not let him have power over her.

I guess this is how my twelve year old brain interpreted romantic feelings. I grew to be offended at any man who felt the need to express his feelings for me and then expect me to respond mutually, just because of how he felt. The connection there is a little twisted, I get that - but I think that for some women, it can be so real. How many times have you watched a girl fall into the trappings of a guy's feelings for her and let it convolute how she processes information? How many times have you been that girl? I know that I have let someone else's feelings for me dictate my motives and actions and that I have sacrificed pieces of who I am to make someone else like me, even love me. Even if it's a committed relationship – the mutual feelings of love and acceptance have to grow from just that – mutual feelings. In the end, it's a healthy perspective of our identity apart from another person's opinion that leads us into

CHAPTER 1: FIRSTS

healthy dating; it's not one person's "yes" that makes a healthy whole.

The summer after sixth grade, I got my first boyfriend. It was that kind of thing where all my friends were doing it, so I thought, "why not?" It was also the summer of discovering late night chat rooms that my parents most certainly would have Ricky Martin-ed, the summer of fresh zits popping up on the landscape of my face, and the summer of growing into the woman I am today, because this kind of awkward charm doesn't grow on trees.

Nick was my crush on and off for the majority of elementary school. He was the one who stood in front of me in every line my classmates and I ever made because our last names were an alphabetical power couple. I'll never forget the one Halloween when the class hottie, Conrad, told us we should go as Barbie and Ken because we looked perfect together. Swoon. Talk about a case of not hating the messenger.

I grew up in that special time when online chatting was the original text message. It's my generation you have to thank for when you get reprimanded for making a phone call because texting is "so much easier." We were the ones who first decided that explaining your true feelings for someone through a typed out computer generated message was the best way to get the full emotional capacity and intentional tone of voice across to the person you felt a deep sense of connection with. That, or we really had a thing for proclaiming mammalian dominance through the use of our opposable thumbs. Jury's still out.

So one night, Nick logged on to instant messenger and sent me the heartfelt chat, "will you go out with me?" My heart started pounding out of my flat 12-year-old chest and my palms grew clammy. I knew the rules. My parents were very clear about no dating until the age of sixteen. But this is what everyone else was doing, so why couldn't I? The only reason I decided on studying my 6th grade instrument was so that Nick could help me get set up every day. I lowered my fingertips over the keyboard and typed out my destiny:

hazelnutcase7: *yes.*

I felt warmth spread through my body – I was officially Nick's girlfriend. Life was amazing. Barbie and Ken had arrived. I had visions of us walking the halls of our separate junior highs, instant messaging about our days...

"How was your day?"

"Good. HBU?"

"Good."

And then it hit me. I was never going to see him again. My bubble of sunshine and girlfriend status popped in my face, replaced by the looming anxiety of the reality of being twelve. We can only get together if our parents drive us places and we live on opposite sides of the city AND I'm technically not allowed to date anyone, so goodbye parents driving us places.

I spent the next two days avoiding my instant messenger, which is the equivalent of today's twelve-year-old going somewhere without their cell phone. Finally, I knew I had to say something, so I logged on. Nick's IM name sat on the right side of my computer screen, unaware of the kind of hurt his next double click would bring. And then, the sound of a door opening. Nick was online. I opened a new chat window and started to reveal my true feelings with fingers that held high scores in all areas of typing quizzes.

"What's up?"

  "NM, how r u?"

  "Good. I'm sorry, but I can't be your girlfriend."

  "You're dumping me?"

  "No, I just can't."

  "Wait, what?"

  "I'm sorry, bye."

CHAPTER 1: FIRSTS

The sound of a door closing.

hazelnutcase7 is away.

And that's how I broke up with my first boyfriend.

I wish I could tell you that we are still friends today. I wish I could say that we eventually got back together when one of us was old enough to drive. I wish I could say our names finally combined and Barbie and Ken lived on forever, but that never happened. I spent the rest of that summer recovering from my drive-by first experience with dating. "Does he hate me now? Will I ever get to really be someone's girlfriend? What will junior high be like without him?"

School was always different for me. Both of my parents were teachers at the high school I attended and my dad was the head football coach, so my last name wasn't exactly unknown. I grew up being "Little Prisk" and couldn't walk into a grocery store without getting recognized. My life was *Friday Night Lights* minus all the drama. I was Hayden Panettiere in *Remember the Titans*. No but actually, we were the Titans. I was the water girl for a high school football team in small town America, where the boys left school for the first day of deer season and my teachers knew more about me than what I cared to share. Mix together an intimidating father and a whole town that knows who you are, and dating gets really complicated. Especially when things like Valentine's Day roll around.

Valentine's Day at our junior high meant carnation sales and awkward love letters from boys who thought that was the perfect day to bring their true feelings out of the woodwork. My first ever experience with carnation sales was equivalent to being caught off guard by a breeze-block falling from the sky. Instead of being quietly available for pick up at the receiver's discretion, these floral representations of affection were unabashedly passed out during 5th period. And as a seventh grader,

I was given 34 carnations. 34 awkward handwritten notes scrawled out on half slips of paper. 34 reasons to turn bright red and want to stuff myself back inside my sixth grade locker. 34 breeze-blocks that I didn't see coming. I felt so bad that 34 people had taken the time to write me a short note and spend one dollar on their feelings for me that I begged my mom to take me to the grocery store after school so I could buy a bag of candy and write out 34 Valentine thank-you notes. I brought them all to school the next day in a plastic grocery bag and handed out the notes one by one, making all the boys who had sent me a carnation very confused. Apparently, I was supposed to just pick and respond to one of them. Dating rules were pretty murky in junior high, if only for the fact that it was junior high, so "dating" meant seeing each other on Friday nights at football games, prank calls from your family's landline, and toilet papering the house of your crush.

Friday nights during football season were like one big poorly chaperoned social event - except for me. I sat perched in the stands, surrounded by loaded opinions of burly men and boisterous women who thought they could do my dad's job better than he could, a career that boasted 27 years of never having a losing season. Instead of walking circles around the football field, kicking up dust and rumors like all the other kids, I always sat huddled next to my mom and sister, wondering what the next play would be; wondering why the quarterback didn't pass or what the referee saw that made him call holding. I would cheer until my throat grew sore and keep a loving hand on my mom's shoulder as she rocked back and forth, praying *Hail Marys* over the tense moments.

All of the kissing that happened under the bleachers on Friday nights was never even on my radar until Monday morning, and by that time, I was too concerned with who we were playing next and how good their quarterback was to care; my family had spent the weekend eating homemade chicken wings and watching game tapes with a side of peanut m&ms, so boys and bleachers were the last thing on my mind.

CHAPTER 1: FIRSTS

    I thought this was normal. But isn't that just like life: you're totally ignorant until you realize that there's another way to do something that you didn't learn from your family. But my aversion to and complete naiveté towards the opposite sex - I'm still trying to figure out where I learned that from.

    My earliest impression of males was that they were obnoxious dummies that chased you around the playground and head-butted your shins while you dangled upside down from the monkey bars. I didn't want anything to do with these flailing balls of energy that roamed around with open mouths - always shoving food in and letting words plop out. So once I decided I would never let them get close to me, it stuck. And I decided that dating was a weakness and I didn't need anyone else to tell me I was pretty. I set my sights on my life goal of running away from home and becoming a child star who rode around in limos and ate ice cream for breakfast.

    Actually, I only tried to run away to Hollywood twice. I would pack my child-sized suitcase full of necessities (my stuffed bunny named Sunny, my P.O.D. CD, our Sam's Club jug of animal crackers) and dream of hitchhiking to Hollywood to become a star. I only ever made it halfway down the driveway before turning around and wandering into the front yard to perform for the garden vegetables and flowers. I had no time or care for romance or boys – until one caught my eye the summer after seventh grade. My first real crush.

    My first and initially most pursued passion was singing. My family used to play this game on road trips where we would listen to a song for five seconds, and once I started singing along, they would change the channel to try and find a song I didn't know.

    I highly doubt it was this moment in time that my parents knew I would grow up taking private voice lessons and dancing competitively, mainly because if they had, they probably would have played the lottery a few more times. Either way, by my thirteenth summer, I was a lanky choral nerd in desperate need of braces who decided that two weeks at Blue Lake Fine Arts Camp were just what I needed. I slept in a drafty cabin with nine other fine arts adolescents that I made connections with over the next fourteen days that I still carry with me to this day. I'll never forget that one of my cabin mate's moms mailed her the latest copy of Harry Potter because it was released while we were away at camp. I begged my mom to send me JK Rowling's latest stories, but no dice. Instead, we would fall asleep as our bunkmate read aloud the adventures of Harry, Ron, and Hermione in *Half Blood Prince*.

Four years earlier, all millennials will remember that the first movie of the Harry Potter franchise was released. Call me a closet bad girl, but my absolute crush from the first movie was Draco Malfoy, played by Tom Felton. A time comes to mind when I had several of my girlfriends over for a sleepover. *Harry Potter* was slipped into the VHS player and as Draco graced the screen, someone hit pause so we could take turns giggling and kissing his Slytherin loving face. My sincerest apologies, Tom.

So at this camp, it came time for the choir to gather together once in the morning and once in the afternoon. I would quietly mind my own business sitting outside in the sun reading mystery novels my dad had pilfered from a thrift store for a quarter before the director would arrive and unlock the door to the choir room. The way the chairs were set up, the sopranos sat across from the basses. There was one singer in the choir who looked exactly like, or as close to as my teenage heart could stand, Draco Malfoy. His bright blonde hair fell loosely over his ears and was further illuminated by the crystal strands of sunshine that fell through the long windows dotting the choral hall. Day by day, I became mesmerized by the *idea* of this Malfoy look-alike without ever saying one word to him.

At the end of the two weeks, the counselors announced that there would be an all-camp dance. We were to attend wearing our uniforms, but we were allowed to wear denim shorts or skirts as opposed to our everyday navy blue bottoms. It was at this point that another boy from the band group of camp approached me and asked if I had a date to the dance. I still wonder if it's because he wanted to take me or because he sincerely wanted to know.

"No, why? Who should I go with?" I asked him.

"Well... who do you want to go with?" Peter asked, possibly hoping to hear his own name.

I immediately gave him the side eye and he knew I had someone in mind.

"There's someone! Tell me who!"

"Ugh, it could never happen," I sighed dramatically. At this point, the nameless bass singer was one hundred percent a magical wizard who attended Hogwarts School of Witchcraft and Wizardry.

"Come on, just tell me! I can hook you up!" Peter persisted. Me and Draco, dreamily dancing away into the night... I wanted in.

"Okay...it's him." I pointed across the cafeteria at Draco, sitting alone at a picnic table. Peter's brown eyes matched the focal point of my finger and opened to the size of dinner plates.

"...Um, him?" Peter turned back to me.

"Yes! Him." Malfoy. Draco Malfoy. Ask him.

"Okay." Peter kept staring at me. "You're sure?"

"Yes. I'm sure." I nodded intently.

"Well okay then. He's one of my cabin-mates. I can ask him for you. If you're sure."

This was it. All my *Princess Diaries* dreams were about to come true. They were staying in the same cabin - it couldn't be a more perfect setup! Peter pressed his palms into the wood of the picnic table bench we were sharing and stood to his feet. With one last look in my direction, he turned toward the table where Draco sat, kicking golden brown wood chips out of his way with each step towards my fairytale future. I felt my hands grow clammy. I couldn't watch. I turned away from the boys and stared out across the lake.

What felt like an hour of daydreaming about attending Hogwarts and shouting spells at each other ended up being thirty seconds of Peter asking his cabin-mate if he wanted to go to the dance with me. I felt the picnic table bench buckle and regroup as Peter re-took the space next to me. I swiveled to face him.

"Well?"

"He wants to go with you." Peter sat hunched forward, elbows on his knees, fingers interlaced. I wondered why he wasn't immediately thrilled for me.

"He does?! Oh my gosh, really?" I tried my best to play it cool and not look over his shoulder at my future dance date.

"Yep," Peter sighed. "He sure does. But you're sure you want to go with him? He can be kind of awkward. I mean, he's a nice guy, but - "

At this point, I started getting offended. What was Peter's problem? He had just done this really nice favor for me and now it was like he was trying to talk me out of it - out of Draco. Plus, who wasn't awkward at 12 years old?

"What do you mean?" Now I was upset. He asked me who I wanted to go with, I told him, and he made it happen. I didn't ask him for advice or relationship guidance.

"Well, he's just..." Peter realized there was no talking me out of it. What was done was done. He let out a puff of air and raised his eyebrows in my direction. "You just let me know how it goes. We're all meeting back here before the dance."

When I got back to my cabin, all the girls were talking about the dance; who they were going with, what music they hoped would play, if the counselors would be there. The girl I'd grown closest to seemed to know everything about boys and life in general, so each time she opened her mouth I clung to her every word.

"Ooh girl," She'd start. "If I could get a date with that bubble butt

CHAPTER 1: FIRSTS

Italian guy who's in the choir with us, that'd be my choice. How did he get a butt like that? It looks fake!"

I knew exactly who she was referring to. He was about five years older than us and sat in the tenor section. He was attractive, but older boys gave me anxiety and the fact alone that he was from another country intimidated the heck out of me. I admired her for her confidence and spunk.

"Yeah, I'm going with Draco," I squeaked out.

"Draco? Who the hell is Draco?"

"You know, Draco Malfoy. The blonde kid who sits in the bass section. Peter is one of his cabin-mates and he asked him if he wanted to go with me."

Hannah leaned away from me and raised her eyebrows.

"Okay girl, if that's who you want," she grimaced.

I was confused. When Peter had tried to crush my Hogwarts dreams, I was offended, but this was someone I considered a true friend questioning my choices. Time to listen up.

"Wait, what do you mean? Should I not go with him?" I was suddenly aware that I may have made the biggest mistake of my young life. I actually started to realize that I didn't even know this kid - we'd never said one word to each other. I wanted to give him the benefit of the doubt, but my benefit was wearing thin.

"Well, I think everyone deserves a chance, you know. He might end up being great." I was hit by the reality that she knew something I didn't.

Later on, as all the girls were getting excited about pairing their denim shorts or skirts with their "I've been at sleep away camp for two weeks" hair, I decided that I was going to suck it up and at least give him a chance. I stepped into my hand-me-down denim skirt and sneakers, linked elbows with my girls, and headed off down the path to the common area escorted by the cheery ringing of camp chants bouncing off the Pine trees.

I'd been sending letters home every day, writing to my parents about all I was learning at camp. Looking back, I know those two weeks were monumental in the way that I now see myself discovering for the first time that beauty wasn't found in perfection, but in raw personality and the vulnerability of new and undetermined friendships. I haven't kept in touch with any of my camp friends from that summer. I followed them on social media for a while, but following them and not actually knowing them anymore felt like a strange invasion of privacy – a privilege I no longer had because we hadn't stayed in touch. But with the meshing of their senses of humor, with their unadulterated conversation topics, with their ability to accept everyone and delegate from a place of honesty and love, they taught me how to be a real human.

I'll always look back on those two weeks with gratitude. I'll always be thankful that this was a chapter in my life; that I got to experience fourteen days at Blue Lake Fine Arts Camp with some truly amazing girls whom I know, given the chance, would become history making women. We didn't all believe in the same religion, and we weren't there to study the same passions, but we never even thought to let our differences divide us and determine for us how we were going to treat each other. That little cabin was magic, and you have to hold onto magic.

Needless to say, the dance that night was entertaining for anyone watching me run from one side of the dance floor to the other, avoiding the boy I'd pedestaled as Draco Malfoy. When we met up at the picnic tables, he proved to be exactly how Peter tried to explain it to me. We danced together for a couple songs, but when he tried to move in closer, I politely told him I wasn't interested. From the way I remember, he got pretty upset, naturally, so I lost him in the sea of blue polos and summer camp hormones. Moral of the story, Tom Felton is not a choral singer from Michigan who spends his summers perfecting his sight singing abilities. The true moral of the story? Your idea and expectations about a person should never convolute the pure truth of who they really are.

CHAPTER 1: FIRSTS

Everyone deserves the opportunity to live free of your pre-meditated expectations, especially when it comes to dating.

2

Chapter 2: It's Not You, It's My Expectations

It's humbling to realize that a large portion of personal disappointment arises from our own unchecked expectations. When I was young, I read the quote by Shakespeare that goes:

> *"Expectation is the root of all disappointment."*

To me, it sounds like Shakespeare had a couple pretty big heartbreaks that he never fully recovered from. To make a blanket statement about expectations yielding all the world's disappointment tells me that he should have had a few more DTR conversations. But, if it's Shakespeare's rotten love life that we have to thank for *Romeo and Juliet,* then we have to give credit where it's due. That, and we've turned years of ancient unrequited romance into hundreds of homework assignments on iambic pentameter.

    The thing that I really do appreciate about Shakespeare's statement is that it calls for one to look at their circumstances with a crisp, even if slightly unwilling, sense of raw honesty. The night of the all-camp dance, I could have blamed my disappointment with the way things turned out on the boy I consistently compared to a fictional character, but

CHAPTER 2: IT'S NOT YOU, IT'S MY EXPECTATIONS

my expectation of him was completely off-base; an expectation I created ignorantly and selfishly. I examined his outward appearance through the lens of my own tunnel-vision and subsequently set an unreasonable set of expectations for this poor boy to live up to. I didn't give him a chance to tell me who he was, and instead assumed that he would fulfill a role in my fantasy world of make-believe.

So often, this is how we treat dating. We selfishly let another person walk into the expectations we have built up for our potential partner. We have to be able to separate who they truly are with the role we think they could play in our lives. No matter how subconscious that thought might be, growing an awareness for these things is crucial.

I believe in setting realistic expectations for your potential life partner, but these expectations have to come out of the place of who they really are so that you can find common ground together. These realistic expectations have to include honoring the other person you're entering into a relationship with without making them feel inadequate or like they need to change any part of themselves to "fit" a role you've created in your mind. I know this changes as the relationship grows. Every healthy marriage has healthy expectations, especially when it comes to commitment, respect, and open communication (among other things). But a healthy expectation for romance and dating is not that the person you sit across from is going to meet each and every one of your dreamt up desires about love *or* your needs. It's not healthy to imagine it all ahead of time before it has played out, either. It's not healthy to expect a fairy tale - you have to make room for real life.

My relationships, romantic or not, began to improve exponentially when I started taking responsibility for my emotional reactions to things and began checking in with my expectations in healthy ways. I stopped expecting my friends to be able to read my thoughts and started communicating more effectively. I stopped seeing other people through the lens of what they could do or be for me and gave them a fighting chance to stand on their own. I stopped getting ahead of myself and walked appropriately and respectfully in stride with the person I had feelings for. So often, the expectations we carry are expressed by our words and actions and the person we are in relationship with ends up suffering the consequences of our unfair unchecked expectations.

After graduating college, I moved out to California. At this time, I was pursuing a life in performing arts and picked up a singing role in a big time performance of a Disney musical. I remember mercilessly staring down the guy cast to play one of the leads until he noticed me. I let our relationship run a quick storyline in my head from start to finish, got up the courage to talk to him, and then walked into one of the most unhealthy relationships to ever exist in my life. The word 'smitten' always had this romantic quality to it before I met Craig, and after we broke up, I promised never to be smitten again.

This was a pattern in my life: I would carry around the idea of a person and a perfect relationship instead of the reality of them. I would want to carry out this storyline before really getting to know them. It came from the place of always hoping for the best in the other person combined with striving after the ideal storyline of engagement, marriage, family I'd grown up anticipating. But letting people be themselves outside of your expectations of invented romance is the freedom that they deserve and the freedom that you deserve. It boils down to loving someone for exactly who they are, warts and all, and not who you expect them to be.

Now in my twenties, dating looks less like fairytales and more like real life, thank goodness. I've finally taken a mature stance on the thin layer of ice that is superficial attraction and stopped letting someone's physical appearance dictate my decisions about who they are and what I think about them. A useful technique is to imagine the person you have feelings for, then imagine if you were talking to them while wearing a blindfold. How does that change your response? We need to be attracted to our significant other, like head-over-heels attracted, but we can't let physical traits dictate how we treat them.

I've spent a great deal of my life working in what can be best generalized as customer service. Over the years, I have learned that customer service is not so much treating people well and going above and beyond for them as it is reading between the lines of what they're saying to find the expectations they had for a specific situation that were not met. It's like being hangry. I've come to recognize that 9 angry times out of 10, I just need a snack. People in my life have learned that when my PH balance drifts into the territory of ornery, it's time to ask Audrey if she's upset or if she's eaten yet today. My goal as an adult is to recognize this mood before it hits and to start communicating, "hey, I'm sorry for being snappy, I just need to go eat something."

Communicating your expectations to people is so good for so many reasons. It sets boundaries, creates intentionality, and levels the playing field by giving people the opportunity to say, "hey, that's an unfair expectation and no one, myself included, is ever going to meet it." It also gives you the chance to speak out what you need, thus giving you and the other person a place of accountability that you can grow from. Communicating your expectations also keeps you from falling for the *idea* of something instead of the reality of it. It's also a great way to measure how healthy your relationship with another person is; are you comfortable communicating expectations? Do you have an intimate enough relationship with this person that you trust them to hold you accountable for communicating expectations that are reasonable? Do you trust them to hold up their end of the relationship? Do you give each other grace when a healthy expectation doesn't get met, and how?

This practice has helped me grow so much not just in my dating life, but in all areas of my life. Whether they were passed onto us by our family dynamics or grown in our minds overtime, the expectations we have need to be communicated and checked. If we're able to say our expectations out loud, we can determine whether they are appropriate or not and then adjust them accordingly. Self-accountability is equally important as staying accountable to the boundaries you have established with another person.

One day in my late twenties, I met this guy at the beach. It was a brisk January day in Southern California (think low 50s) and we were both there to watch a casual beach volleyball tournament. We had both brought our favorite snacks, his being Cheez-Its and mine being crackers with smoked salmon dip, and we shared our food as we talked about our mutual love for pineapple pizza and chocolate chip cookie dough ice cream. We talked about our favorite ways to spend free time and discovered that we had matching jagged scars on the clefts of our chins - his from a fall while skateboarding, mine from getting a little careless one New Year's Eve (I was eight and playing with the cat; one game of "chase" and a countertop later, I was in the emergency room before the clock struck midnight). Needless to say, we had a lot in common, and the list just kept growing as we talked through his favorite movies, gymnastic routines, and skatepark maneuvers. Eventually, he looked up at me sporting an orange gatorade mustache and said through a mouthful of Cheez-Its, "we should go to the skatepark together sometime."

"Totally!" I said back. "That'd be so fun. Let me ask your dad first though..."

Hopefully, things got weird for you around the Gatorade mustache. But yes, he was nine, and my ideal in every way. Except that he was nine. Later that night, he (his dad) paid for my fries at In'N Out and I knew in my heart that he had just set the bar high for any potential future boyfriend.

I love the simplicity that conversation brought me back to; the simplicity of, "Hey, you like the things that I like even though we're two completely different people, so we should hang out sometime and do those things."

CHAPTER 2: IT'S NOT YOU, IT'S MY EXPECTATIONS

So often, we put pressure on other things in relationships. We put pressure on the romance, the sweeping off of feet, the serious future things. But when you're just getting to know someone and even after you've been together for 40 years, that's what's important: carefree timelessness with them talking about and doing the things you like to do together. I've had to learn the hard way that relationships require a foundation of 'best friendship' for anything else to flourish. I understand that not everyone is the same or lives life at the same pace, but I'd rather be with someone who holds the first chair in friendship before things get all lovey-dovey.

John Mayer has said this best in a live recording of *Tracing* off of his as/is album. I would write it out for you here, but I'm doing my best to avoid any sort of copyright infringement. So let's treat this like a multimedia experience, shall we? Go ahead, take a minute to listen. I'll be right here when you get back.

What makes you gaga for someone has to be who they are, it cannot be about your heart eyes blinding you based upon years of romantically dreamt up scenarios. It cannot be your idea of your future with them, because the future doesn't exist yet.

There are so many things that we use to create this false narrative for someone because we think they're cute or we like their accent or we have a crush on them for another heart-fluttering reason, but if we force a relationship out of these things, it's like planting a sunflower in shallow soil. These are not the things that bring about longevity and intentionality. If you have a crush on someone because of exactly who they are, warts and all, *that's* how it should be. If you have a crush on them because you already know them and that they take their eggs over easy because they like dipping bread into their runny yoke or because they laugh and then they snort and then milk comes out their nose every time they hear Dane Cook stand up even though the 2000s were like so long ago, *that* should be why you have a crush on them, not these falsely created ideas that you have attached feelings to. That's backwards.

Ultimately, our life is made up of our own choices. Not just our choices, but our motives behind our choices. One choice has one million other reasons and leitmotifs behind it, and if you're not choosing someone because of their current reality, then why are you choosing them? Your choice to say 'yes' or 'no' to adding someone into your life, especially romantically, has to be because of their reality, which means, who they are right here and right now and also who you are. They're worthy right now, so how can you love your fullest in this moment?

Obviously, I am guilty of projecting my romantically invented expectations on unassuming gentlemen just trying to get better at their vocal practices. I have been more than willing to let my fantasies dictate who someone is to me instead of letting that person's actions, life, and words show me and tell me who they are. There is a fine line that exists between having a healthy and beautiful hope for your future without dragging other people into your own personal twilight zone.

If we leave our expectations unchecked, the danger is that we end up dragging other people into our relationships embedded with fantastical notions, causing an even bigger mess. While there's plenty of grace for our mess, there's also the better option of dealing with the things we carry around before setting them on someone else's shoulders and asking them to do life with us.

3

Chapter 3: Vulnerability

I thought up one million different ways to give you an anecdote on vulnerability and out of all of them, I couldn't shake this one:

One early May morning, I boarded a 737 at the Pittsburgh airport with a handful of other college students. My suitcase weighed in barely under the allowed 50 pounds and I settled myself into the narrow confines of a middle seat in aisle 17, squished between a total stranger and another one of my International Media Studies classmates. We'd spent the semester studying media outlets in Europe, and were on our way to Rome for two weeks of pizza and gelato disguised as tours through newsrooms and blog post requirements.

Let me interrupt by saying that the night before, my friends had all gathered for a farewell dinner party, and since I was leaving the next morning for Italy, pasta and red wine were heavily consumed. Up until this point in my life, believe it or not, I had never experienced the devastating effects of a hangover. I had seen disheveled party-goers grab their foreheads and sulk by the toilet bowl, but I was never able to commiserate with them, until this day.

It snuck up on me in a way best described by a line from my favorite movie, *Funny Girl*. Fanny Brice, played by Barbara Streisand, says,

"Suppose all you ever had for breakfast was onion rolls, and then one morning, in walks a bagel. You'd say, 'Ugh, what is that?' Until you tried it!"

My red wine hangover was a bagel on a plate full of onion rolls. That morning, I woke up too early to notice what was wrong. Adrenaline for my first ever international trip was pumping strongly through my dehydrated body systems. But then, my electrolyte imbalance really reared its ugly head on the flight from Pittsburgh to Philadelphia when the pilot decided that to land safely, we needed to play a 45 minute game of tag with the cumulus clouds surrounding us. Turbulence started and never stopped as we flew from one Pennsylvanian city to the next and I knew it wasn't going to end well for me.

Calmly, I turned toward my classmate and rested a hand on her forearm. Not twenty minutes earlier, she was giddy as a child on Christmas morning gazing out the window of her very. First. Plane ride.

"I'm so sorry, but I think I'm going to be sick," I said to her as I reached for the airline provided barf bag, opened it up, and set it in front of my mouth. I spent the rest of our wrenching descent and landing hunched forward in my seat, cupping the growing contents of my barf bag. When it was all over with, I rolled the top of the bag down and set it gently in my lap, knowing there was no way I was going to pass it off to a poor unsuspecting flight attendant.

Vulnerability is looking a stranger dead in the eye on their very first ride in an airplane and telling them that you're about to barf in front of them, and then proceeding to barf in front of them. To top it all off, this lovely classmate spent my barfing episode with her hand patting my back, telling me it was going to be okay.

I was told once we landed that no one around me really knew what was happening and that my subtle barfing really just looked like a set of sneezes. Looking back, I think I remember someone offering up a

CHAPTER 3: VULNERABILITY

"bless you" at one point. Either way, I learned the hard way that morning to always drink water with your wine. I spent the entirety of the eight hour flight to Rome passed out across multiple seats, complete with an eye mask and airline blanket. When I cracked an eyelid somewhere around Eastern France, I discovered that the elderly Italian man in the next closest seat to me had requested that the flight attendant leave a blueberry muffin on my tray table for when I came to. I'll probably mention him at my wedding; my grandchildren will hear stories about this man. Hopefully, he will read this book one day and smile.

    The thing is, sometimes we have to go to the place that we don't want to go to as our only option. That day on the plane, I could have run up to the bathroom gagging and no one would have ever been the wiser, except the seatbelt sign was on and I was wedged between people in a middle seat, leaving me with the most vulnerable option. It's never comfortable and it's never our first choice, but it's so necessary if we want to make it to the really really good stuff. And if you're wondering what's really good about barfing into a bag on an airplane, take this book as your example.

    One high school summer, I was absolutely hung up on one of my cousin's friends. He was older than me, had sunny blonde hair and this boyish grin that made my knees weak. His mom was always coming up to me in church with strange questions about my personal life that made me think she was on to me.

    One beautifully golden summer evening, Steve came over to my cousin's house. He was newly sixteen and I couldn't drive, so the fact that he had a car made him all the more appealing. My cousin, ever the encouraging friend, suggested that we all leave the gathering the adults were enjoying for a round of mini golf. I started sweating. Sweating is my immediate response to anything thrilling or nerve-wracking. I thought that my cousin was trying to set us up. This sweet next of kin was doing his best to get me a night out with my ultimate crush.

The three of us approached the group of parentals lazily sipping beers in the summer heat.

"Hey, can we head out to play mini golf?" My cousin asked. His mom tended to be more lenient than mine.

"Sure, but who's going to drive?" Good point, Aunt Elle.

"Steve – he drove here," my favorite cousin cooly responded.

"Fine with me, just check with Audrey's parents first."

I choked. Three teenagers in the car with a new driver, my parents would never go for it. They had rules about that. They had rules about everything. He looked over at me with his lips sucked in. We walked over to my parents and proposed the same question.

"Well, who's driving?" my mom asked, like any good parent should.

"Steve is," I said through the haze of my bright red cheeks.

My mom looked over to where Steve stood – six feet tall, fresh biceps – she was not about to be fooled by me.

"You can go if Marshall sits in the front seat. And let me get Steve's cell phone number," she slyly responded.

Mortified. I was mortified. His cell phone number?! Like she was going to call and check up on us?! Though heavily embarrassed, I looked over at Steve, who had heard the whole conversation.

"Sure!" Steve walked over to my mom and flipped open his phone, gaining cool points by the millisecond. Everything was going to be okay. We were going to make it. But then, my dad turned around. He peered over my mom's shoulder as she exchanged numbers with Steve, took a gulp of his beer, and said nonchalantly to my crush, "yeah, you can drive."

My eyes widened. I looked up at my dad, the world's most intimidating man, and watched as a shimmering halo formed around his head. I thought for sure he was turning around to put a stop to the whole thing, but he gave the final go-ahead.

"But," he continued, staring Steve straight in his eyes, "if you're

CHAPTER 3: VULNERABILITY

driving and get in an accident and my daughter gets one single scratch, just know that I'm not afraid to kill you and bury you in my backyard."

The angel chorus choked on their hallelujah. I felt the air rush out of my chest as time stopped and I melted into a puddle on the floor from the heat of embarrassment.

Kill him?! *Bury* him?! In that moment, I wished that I was the one being put out of her misery. I closed my eyes, afraid to even look in Steve's direction. Even Mr. Cool couldn't withstand something like that. Sure enough, Steve had turned bright red. He mumbled something about being safe and reached out to shake my dad's hand. My dad dipped his chin, smiled, and knew he had successfully kept one more guy from laying hands on his youngest daughter.

We all managed to escape that night under the embarrassing cloud of my parent's discipline. Mini golf was a blast, but I quickly realized that Steve thought of me more as the little sister type and less like the dateable type. That, or my dad's final comments got under his skin enough to prevent him from exploring the latter option any further. There was a rumor floating around at one point that Steve wanted to ask me to homecoming, but that he was too afraid of my dad to follow through. I don't blame the guy.

Steve was one of the more serious crushes that I had during my young life - I secretly hoped that, one day, I would hear from him again, because he was my ideal in every way - or so my teenage self imagined.

When we develop crushes, they're like a smoldering teepee of sticks just waiting for a brush with lighter fluid. It's this undeniable sensation that makes us drowsy in real life and partial to a specific person - a person we could either know a little or not at all. Crushes give us an emotional expectation - whether spoken or unspoken - that we are responsible for managing.

I'm 27 writing this and I still tell my crush's how I feel about them. Most of you are like, "yeah, and notice how you're still single?" But I couldn't do it any other way - I'm like a walking sign post of emotions. People know the second I'm feeling any kind of way because I can't wipe it off my face, my mood, or my sleeves. If it doesn't come out of my mouth, I carry it like a valentine burning a hole in my pocket until I can't stand it any longer. It must come out, otherwise I find myself doing and saying things totally out of character. For me, the only real way to manage my emotional state is to be vulnerable. Games are overrated. Games hurt people and keep emotions on the fringe. Games encourage mysterious behavior and shut out freedom like window panes in winter. And no healthy relationship ever survived without freedom. But the only way to get on the path of enjoying freedom in our relationships is through vulnerability.

Fighting vulnerability is like building a Berlin Wall separating joy from the things you're truly hoping for in life, because no joy is ever complete without vulnerability and no relationship is complete without it either. It's going to find us whether we specifically choose it, like choosing a barf bag, or whether it chooses us, like a spontaneously arranged mini golf session with a childhood crush. In my 20-some years of experience, I've found that it's better to just choose vulnerability and get it over with. Because in choosing vulnerability, we are also choosing intentionality.

Intentionality tells the person at the receiving end of your affection, "you're important to me, you matter to me, you're special to me, and I see your true worth." It can be hard to say that to someone, because it means we open up, but what's the point in living a life where we're closed up like an ocean clam? Where's the vibrancy in that? It also goes the other way - when we know that our relationship with someone needs to come to an end, we have to intentionally talk to them about it.

The amazing Brené Brown did a study on vulnerability and concluded that the only way true connection happens is when people allow themselves to be really seen, and no concept has ever spoken to me more. She goes on to explain that being "really seen" can be hard for some of us because it calls upon courage. I believe in a healthy and regular expression of courage. Here's my personal definition:

Courage: to tell the story of who you are with your whole heart.

We can't practice compassion for other people unless we have kindness for ourselves. And kindness means making sure we are *whole* - making sure that when we interact with others, it's not in a selfish way that leaves them jaded, or in a way that asks them to be emotionally or physically responsible for *our* choices. It's acting from a place of purified love instead of acting with the hope of receiving love. Choosing kindness calls on courage because the world tells us to pick another option. "Pick cynicism, indifference, or pride," it says. But try this on for size: Brené also taught me that the root word for courage comes from the latin word *cor*, which means *heart*. So, let your courage bring you into vulnerability and your vulnerability bring you into intentionality. We have the power to choose these things; we owe the world our purest motive and bravest choice.

> *"...for God gave us a spirit not of fear, but of power and love and self-control." 2 Timothy 1:7 ESV*

4

Chapter 4: Worthiness

I love pancakes. Growing up, one of the ways my dad used to make sure he would get quality time with his daughters was by making us breakfast every morning, usually in the form of blueberry pancakes. With some convincing, those blueberries occasionally became chocolate chips.

This kind of quality time will always be incredibly meaningful to me. I loved hanging out with dad at breakfast as a kid. But notice how I also just said that I love pancakes. I used the same word to describe my feelings about two completely different things; one was quality time with a parent, the other, an inanimate object that passes through my digestive system and turns into poop. I compared poop to cherished memories.

So how do we differentiate between the two? It seems ridiculous that I'm even posing this question to be taken seriously, but I'm the one writing the book, not you. Welcome to my Matrix.

What's required is that we have to use more descriptive vocabulary. We have to take the time to make sure that whoever we're talking to knows that poop-cakes are not equivalent to time with them. Or ice cream. Or overcast weather. Or your favorite holiday. Or 1967 Chevrolet trucks. In

CHAPTER 4: WORTHINESS

this sense, love does not equal love. So, when we tell another person that we love them, how do they know that we're not just comparing them to pancakes and ice cream? How does the other person know that our emotion towards them is more meaningful than our emotion towards food or weather or good news? It's the truth about their worth, and simultaneously, our worth, that fails to be expressed by a word we use to describe our feelings for hundreds of other things.

We have an innate desire to belong and to be loved. It's my belief that we were intentionally created this way, to derive the most we possibly can out of life through relationship and vulnerability while believing fullness of life is found when we believe in the truth of our own self-worth. If we don't subscribe to the full knowledge of our own worthiness before entering into a relationship with another person, we're asking that other person to do something for us that we haven't yet done for ourselves. We rely on them to meet a need that isn't their responsibility to meet. Instead of a process that's meant to be fun and healthy and full of connection, trying to date another person turns into the incessant and harmful question, "am I enough for you?" When we ask other people this question without a prerequisite foundation of self love and acceptance, aka self-worth, we're susceptible to the danger of running after hits of dopamine that are so readily available from "likes," meaningless flirting, and more, which can lead to running from relationship to relationship in the hopes that we'll eventually find ourselves and our happiness. If we don't believe in and truly know our worth simply standing on our own two feet, dating becomes treacherous. Dating turns into deep wells of insecurity asking to be filled by affection from another because the question of belonging has been answered by another person's affirmation before our own.

Answering the questions of belonging and worthiness with our own 'yes' first tears down walls of insecurity, allowing for the ability of *worth without question*. Worth without question prevents settling, insecurity, and silence.

When I was in my early 20s, I lost track of my sense of worth and belonging. I wanted this other person to accept me so badly that I settled in silence for a relationship I knew in my heart of hearts wasn't healthy. Love should feel like ultimate freedom, not like suffering quietly to keep someone around. Maybe this lesson was easy for everyone else to learn, but maybe not. It was in this relationship that I gave the most of myself in ways I can never get back. There are things that to this day I find myself having to make peace with all over again because I tried to find my worth in a relationship that never should have been, all because I didn't think I was worthy of anything different. All because one person told me I belonged with them and I wasn't strong enough to see the great big world that existed beyond his acceptance of me. I gave in to living out of a false sense of worthiness. I let him tell me who I was instead of already knowing, without a doubt, that I was worth loving all on my own. And because of that, I stayed attached to this person for way too long.

But thankfully, truth always breaks through. The truth of our worth, like grace, is not elusive, but it does require our agreement with it to really take hold. When I finally agreed that my worth did not hang in the balance of his words or thoughts about me, I was able to see clearly that I was allowing myself to be treated as less-than because I was failing to believe I was more-than. Do not ever under any circumstances allow anyone to treat you like you are less-than. Better yet, don't ever let anyone's treatment of you declare your worthiness. Believe it first, and that's a foundation they can't take away from you. Believe it first, and the relationship requirement becomes their treatment of you falling in line with the truth of your pre-established identity.

And now, a sidebar.

CHAPTER 4: WORTHINESS

All The Children I'll Never Have

On the eve of my 28th birthday, I started thinking about my eggs… yes, those eggs. Like, really thinking about them. Not because I was getting older or anxious about having kids, but because of the science that says women are born with all the eggs ever to be released in our lifetime. I also started participating in a fertility app - not because I was trying to get pregnant, but out of sheer curiosity of how *everything* in my life was somehow someway connected to my menstrual cycle and these 500 or so microscopic cells that have the capacity to form 50% of a human. I thought about how I'd been releasing an egg once a month every month for the past 16 years, totaling 192 eggs set free to float the crimson tide, give or take a few months of high intensity sports activity. Not only that, but I learned through this app that every single egg that was eventually released to be fertilized (also, ew) had to prove itself dominant over all the other eggs. I wondered if God had a purpose for those eggs that didn't make it or if they were all just placebo. It made me realize that every life created is truly so purposeful and intentional, whether we ourselves intended it to be made or not.

When I was in 6th grade, I would sometimes avoid taking the bus home (can you blame me?) and opt for walking to my mom's office on certain afternoons. One of these days, I left my mom's desk not feeling quite like my normal 12-year-old self and headed for the bathroom. It was there that it happened. As I pulled down my princess Fruit of the Looms, I discovered menstrual terror waiting for me. Having an older sister, I knew what a period was, but never applied that same destiny to myself. Until right at this moment, when my heart started pounding and my hands started shaking, did I realize I was not immune to womanhood. With those same trembling fingers, I hastily wrapped low grade toilet paper around the crotch of my underwear and gathered the courage to share with my mom the bleeding surprise that had just marked my life forever changed.

I was silent in the car the entire drive home. Small tears stung the corners of my eyes as I mourned the loss of my childhood. As much as I had tried to ignore the unavoidable, I had been smacked upside my face with the hard truth; I was becoming a woman and there was nothing that my boy-hating self could do about it.

I zoned out the whole way through my mom's explanation of what was going on in my body. I felt trapped in a delicate box with an unwanted surprise that was tied with a bright red bow. My focus snapped to attention just in time to hear my mom say, "so today, that means you had an egg!" To which I blubbered back, "but I don't want an egg!"

An *EGG*. Like I was a baby chick who couldn't hide behind her mother hen anymore, fresh meat for the local rooster. I couldn't eat eggs for a while after that conversation because every time I did, the image of cracking it onto the crotch of my underwear came to mind.

Reminiscing back on my first egg and thinking through to now, I can't help but notice how women have a tendency to want to put their trust in things like eggs and derive their worth out of words like pregnant, fertility, trying, or mom. Because however it happens or doesn't happen for you, your worth is not derived there. Worth is not something made greater by labels or life moments, no matter which ones they are. Cut us open and you get the same breakdown. It all goes back to the foundation of truth: you are worthy as you are, where you are. If everything was taken from you, your value and your worth would not change or diminish. End sidebar.

When I was a junior in college, I had a fifty-something year old man offer to be my sugar daddy. It was a spring day in Pittsburgh and I was sitting outside enjoying the sunshine, writing thank-you cards from my recent birthday, when an older gentleman sitting at a table not far from me started making conversation. Now when I say older, I mean similar

CHAPTER 4: WORTHINESS

to my father's age, which was 53 at the time. He introduced himself and learned that I was hoping to intern at one of the local magazines for a semester. Coincidentally, he knew one of the editors at one of these magazines and offered to set up an interview. We exchanged emails and I went on my way.

A couple weeks later, potential sugar daddy reached out to set up a time for us to grab coffee so he could "get my resume and send my information to his friend." We met at a Starbucks close to campus and I immediately realized something strange was going on. His three-piece suit had been traded in for perfectly tailored dark-wash denim and he was sporting a diamond encrusted Rolex that sparkled on his wrist as he flicked through a wad of twenty dollar bills that he retrieved from his pocket to pay for his black coffee. I declined his offer to pay for my coffee feeling like I wanted to owe this man as little as possible at the end of whatever was happening.

We sat down and I quickly thanked him and brought up the internship at the local magazine. He sent his editor friend a quick text, emailed her my resume, and proceeded to ask me if I had a boyfriend, how old he was, what we liked to do together, and if I had ever considered dating an older man.

"You're only two years older than my son - he's a nice looking guy too!" He chuckled, seemingly unaware that to my *horror*, he had suggested his son would have to get over his dad dating someone closer to his age.

"What do you like to do? We can go to a Penguins' game, go out for seafood or steak, your choice, and box seats of course..."

By this point, I was in shock. I couldn't believe that this mortgage broker and dad of two was trying to pick up a barely 22 college student.

"Wow, um, what do I say... I'm sorry, but no thank you."

I had reached the point of trying to stay polite while being completely offended. Not only did this man just finish asking incredibly personal questions about my boyfriend, but it also seemed like he didn't care that

I had one and still wanted to throw his hat in the ring. This was the kind of guy I'd seen in movies, but never actually experienced. This was the kind of guy that defined a woman's worth by her worth to him and I could only take so much.

"Thank you for meeting me today, but I will never go on a date with you and I want to be clear that I would like to keep our relationship strictly professional," I said.

Or at least, something to that effect. All I remember is that I laid out a very clear boundary that I could hold him accountable to and made my feelings incredibly clear. It made me sad to think that some women would fall for his flattery and shallow opinion on what she had to offer the world. It made me even more sad to know that he was bringing up children under this mindset while living his life in a position to give so much more. Needless to say, I never heard about an internship.

This world makes it so easy for us to derive our worthiness from things that truly lack the authority to define us. The only acceptable idea that can give luminous color to the truth of our worth is this: loved beyond measure. When we make the daily choice to walk in that truth, the impermanence that exists in everything else in this world becomes clearer and we no longer strive to feel worthy by attaching ourselves to a job, a person, a label, etc; for the sake of worth. There are great things we have the ability and opportunity to do with our lives, but those great things do not provide our worth to us. Worthiness is a fact that everything else gets to spring forth form, not the treasure waiting for us at the end of the map. Anything that's keeping you from knowing that you are worthy as you are right now is a straight up lie.

Something that I've found helpful for myself is to write down all the lies I'm currently believing about myself. They usually sound something like:

I'm not fun to be around

CHAPTER 4: WORTHINESS

    I don't have anything to offer these people
    I have to be funnier for them to like me
    I have to be more to be enough
    I'm only worth loving if...
    Because they rejected me, I'm not worth loving
    Their "yes" affirms my worthiness
    I need him/her to like me

After I've pulled all of those ugly black slugs out of my soul (so *Stranger Things*, I know) I replace them with the truth in hopes of cancelling out the lies forever:

I am allowed to come as I am and be fun or not
    I am irreplaceable and unique – there is no one like me
    I am worthy of love and belonging *as I am*
    I am more than enough
    I am worthy of love in this moment and always
    Their opinion of me does not determine my worthiness
    They also say "yes" to horseradish on their french fries, so their "yes" isn't that great after all...

That last one was more of a personal jab, but you get the picture. The bottom line is, the way that we approach and accept our worthiness determines the way we are able to love ourselves and others. When we know what we ourselves are worthy of and why, we can easily transfer that same truth to the other people in our lives. This truth is everlasting, so the stronger our stance is on this truth, the more we are able to love people from a whole, grounded place.

5

Chapter 5: High School

One of the most awkward dates I've ever been on took place during my sophomore year of high school. It was with a boy in my economics class who, though he would never become the president of the United States, sure talked like he knew how to get there. He was attractive in a lanky-sophomore-in-high-school way, but I never could get over the "know it all" style with which he admonished the political system and all its participants.

He offered to pick me up from home one Sunday afternoon in the throes of winter. He rounded the last bend of my family's driveway to find my father butchering freshly hung venison; cutting out tenderloin and separating ground meat from steaks. My dad, ever the friendly outdoorsman, walked over to Zeke to shake his hand with his butcher knife in the other. Zeke stood his ground instead of running scared back down the driveway and promised to have me home in a couple of hours. While we were getting into his car, my dad yelled an apology for getting deer blood on Zeke's hand. That was our first and last date.

The first time I ever held a boy's hand, I was a junior in high school. He and I were sitting in his car talking after school one day and he asked me if we could hold hands. At this point, I knew I liked hanging out with

CHAPTER 5: HIGH SCHOOL

him, but I was so inexperienced that he actually had to teach me how to hold hands and I couldn't even think about doing anything further - it made me too squeamish. I supposed I did dating backwards, starting with a marriage proposal and 12 years later arriving at hand holding, but I wouldn't have it any other way.

My palms started sweating as he reached for my hand. Out of habit, I grabbed his palm and cupped my fingers tightly around it. He started laughing and, with his opposite hand, peeled my death grip loose and said, "when you hold hands with someone you like, you interlace your fingers, like this."

I remember how weird and uncomfortable it felt, like toe spacers after a pedicure. I remember the butterflies flapping their wings in my stomach, but what I don't remember is the knowledge that while he was acting on his feelings towards me, I was experiencing feelings different from his, even though that's exactly what was happening. I was experiencing thrill, affirmation, connection - but not genuine affection. I wasn't yet emotionally intelligent enough to know the difference, but I'm thankful that my body language portrayed it for me. Because I didn't have romantic feelings for handhold number one, I never acted like I did, probably much to his dismay and definitely much to his decision later on to date someone else.

Some people find their life partners in high school. And when I say some people, I'm really referencing the movie *He's Just Not That Into You*, because these people are the exception, not the rule. When I was in high school, I was given the rule of "no dating until you're sixteen." And while I moped over guys like the best of them, looking back, I'm thankful for that boundary. I'm thankful to have had the subconscious reminder that connecting your life with another person's wasn't an extra-curricular activity, but something designed to be taken seriously. I don't mean serious like twelve-inches-apart-at-all-times-leaving-room-for-Jesus serious, but this boundary established by my parents paved the way for me to develop a healthy perspective; one that was there for me as a reminder that I wasn't ready for dating until I was older. I'd have plenty of time to screw it up after puberty.

Now that I am older, I've had to unlearn some things. Yes, it's healthier for you and the other person to date from a place of truly knowing yourself, but when it came down to the relationship I'd always wanted, I took it way *too* seriously. Dating should be fun. Dating should be like going to a carnival filled with all your favorite rides and foods. You put in the necessary work of knowing what you want to see and eat ahead of time, then you buy the tickets. You meet someone at the entrance. You go on the ferris wheel together and experience each other's favorite ride. Maybe you let them buy you a slice of pizza and you treat them to dessert. When it gets scary, you hold hands. When the pizza comes back up after the Tilt-A-Whirl, they hold your hair away from your face. They're scared of heights, so you wave at them from the top of 1001 Nights. While they shoot out the tin cans, you cheer them on. Even if they don't win the big stuffed unicorn, you hug them anyway and hold their hand the whole way out of the park. Maybe while you're at the carnival, you don't like the way they cut the lines or treat the people working at the booths. If that's the case, then they're probably not the person for you, and that's okay. Maybe while you're on a ride, they take selfies the whole time and tell you not to put your arms up. Then, they're probably not your person and that's still okay. It's that moment where you walk out of the park and realize that even while the pizza was making its final encore, you were enjoying your time with them - that's the stuff you take seriously.

There's a meeting in the middle. There's the knowledge of who you are and what you believe in, the qualities you desire in another person, and the coming together of those things. I understand and respect that every story has its own timeline and storyline, but for me, the reason I even set foot into the dating pool is because of the knowledge that I want to be married one day. It's not to make me whole or complete my life or fill my time, it's because I know that my life's purpose of living out my faith will be made better and stronger by combining my life with another person. I also get to celebrate my time of singleness before that happens, a concept that, as a high schooler, I had zero capacity for grasping. So while dating should be fun and filled with the experience of getting to know another person, it should also be done from a place of intention. And when we're young, that intention isn't always fully developed.

As a teenager, feelings took the shape of mixed cds, flirting in the parking lot after school, and riding down the road singing your favorite songs at the top of your lungs. Those are the sweet experiences where we get to really know the things worth living for; the things that teach us the childlikeness that true love should possess. As we grow, we complicate it. We make it about sex and pride and power. We make it about getting the last word and getting what we think we deserve. We weigh love down with worry and expectation. While I know that I was not in a place to date appropriately while I was in high school, I know that there is a delight to being young that we have to hold on to as we grow, because that's what keeps us authentic and able to love vulnerably and wisely. That's what keeps our perspective of the little things really being the big things. But I've come to realize that our current culture has a tendency to perpetuate the complicated mindset about dating, especially in the world of online dating.

6

Chapter 6: Modern Dating and Special-Order Fiancés

As I started off the latter half of my twenties as an unexpectedly single person recovering from a broken engagement, I discovered that the rumors were true: dating was hard, uncomfortable work. I spent time intentionally choosing to be single, letting wounds heal and getting back to my whole self. But once I knew I was ready and healthy enough to let another person in, I was overwhelmed by the lack of mediums through which I could meet someone and equally upset by my remaining options. So, I made a dating profile.

Have you ever tried to describe yourself to a total stranger using five carefully selected photographs of yourself and a bio short enough for the top of your resume? Actually, if you're reading this and you're a millennial, there's a high chance you've done that. It sucks. Add in a nostalgically romantic take on life, and you get a dangerous concoction of misplaced hope.

First, you have to be up front about asking people what they're even on the app looking for: actual dating, meek conversation, or hooking up. I got the sense from asking around beforehand that this is the norm for all dating apps. But where is the line? I'm here not only wondering if you're interested in actually dating, but I also need to know if you're gainfully employed, drug free, have kids, want kids, going through a divorce, still married, religiously affiliated, and what harmful habits you may or may not have. How am I supposed to fit all those questions in my bio?

I have this theory that our generation is really bad at dating because we've been taught that there is always something better coming (I mean, we're called Generation Ex, for crying out loud). There's always a new upgrade, there's always someone else we can pass our problems off to, and if something's broken, we just go out and get a new one. But that's just it - we miss the mark when it comes to intentionality and commitment. We're always wanting something better, so we fail to see the goodness of what's in front of us from all possible angles.

My parents have been married for 37+ years. Before you get annoyed, I am not by any means saying that this is everyone's path, so just hear me out. They have been married for longer than our generation has been alive, and it's not because the years have been kind to them. It's because they have made choices in response to their circumstances and stood by those choices.

In a culture where we swipe without saying a word and expect what our parents have nurtured for three decades, our choice is more powerful than ever before. I know you've heard everyone say that, but our power grows stronger when we use our ability to choose on the side of intentionality. Intentionality can be scary because it makes us feel vulnerable, but it also allows us to date in healthy ways. Thanks to dating apps, we create a profile and deal with multiple responses from multiple people instead of choosing just one person and focusing on them. We receive free attention and crave more of it. We have constant access to shallow affirmation. It feels good to be wanted and admired. It feels good to know somebody, or even a few someone's, are interested in you.

Like I said earlier, it feels good to seek out that hit of dopamine. But this feeling is rooted in the desire to be loved and wanted, not necessarily known, and once we learn and believe that we're already loved beyond measure, beyond what any other human could possibly express to us, we stop sacrificing intentionality for the sake of shallow attention.

Ultimately, the goal of being with someone is to continue to build on what you started with, right? There's a reason that wedding vows originally included and still include the phrase "til death do us part." It's about the only time the thought of death becomes this romantic vision of you and your true love only existing if it's hand in hand, cheek to cheek, side by side in your rocking chairs on the front porch watching the sunset. I'm not going to bash divorce here. I'm not going to talk about rates or reasons, because I've seen the ending of marriages leave both people better off. I believe that divorce is something that requires us to respect one another's opinion concerning when and why, and not force another person to agree with us. At the end of the day, the only person whose opinion on divorce that should matter aside from yours is your significant other's because I can't think of a more important thing you have to be on the same page about if you plan to get married. There are so many things to talk about before walking down the aisle and saying "I do," SO many things, and this is one of them. You have to be able to talk about what happens when your choice to do life with this person you are choosing is tested in the face of adversity.

But this is why being intentional with the people in our lives, especially when it comes to dating, is so important. This is why we take the time to be intentional with ourselves before choosing to do so with another person. It's a quality that will bleed into all that we do and empower us to become more certain of our own identity *apart from another person*.

It only took me 26 years to decide to live, date, and handle other people's romantic feelings with honesty and intentionality instead of running away and shutting myself inside of a school locker.

CHAPTER 6: MODERN DATING AND SPECIAL-ORDER FIANCÉS

In my dating app phase, I went on a few dates with a really great guy. We had a lot in common, but we also had a lot not in common, foundationally speaking. I'm by no means saying a relationship that is not built on a mutual foundation can't last because I think there are exceptions to that rule. I do know though that for myself, I have to have the same moral, personal, and ethical foundations as the person I want to be in a romantic relationship with. And this guy and me, we didn't have those.

We had an awesome time together, but whenever I was with him, I would feel like we were puzzle pieces that looked like they went together, but if you tried to build the whole jigsaw with them, you'd get far into it only to realize that at some point, you placed the wrong piece in the wrong spot. So finally, I was honest. I knew myself, I knew what I needed, and that my needs not being met by our relationship never once took away from how amazing of a person he was. So before we got too far, I said:

"I believe that the most respectful thing I can do is be honest with you and with myself that we don't fit. I could ignore what I know to be true about myself, or I could act out of pure emotion and keep seeing you, even though I know it isn't honest. You are amazing and a really special guy, but I don't want to lead you on, so I have to take a step back."

I'm the kind of person who recognizes the collateral damage and resounding effect of something the moment it happens. I don't need to play it out or "wait and see" because the answers are all right there. I haven't always been this way. I wish that I was. I've only ever ended things with someone with this much intentionality and respect twice once I finally started maturing, but I wish it's what I would have said every time I needed to. It's recognizing that the other person has so much to offer, but that it has to be offered to someone else for it to truly be fulfilled.

One December night, met up with some girlfriends at a bar downtown after traveling back home to Michigan from Pennsylvania. We're not the wild kind, but we love to have a good time together, especially when reminiscing about high school memories. So, on that night, we ran into a few old friends and had drinks with them, laughing about how we acted in our younger years. I broke away from the conversation to take a walk through the second half of the bar, and on my way back, a distantly familiar voice called my name. Holding half an IPA, I turned to see a tall, dark, and handsome man resting both elbows on top of the bar, leaning back, and smiling at me. The sixth grade king.

"Parker!?"

I gracefully tried to pick my jaw up off the floor as I walked over to him. It had been close to ten years since we had seen each other face to face, and the years had been good to him. I pretended that I wasn't shocked that he called me out of the crowd, like it was the most natural thing in the world that we were about to have a conversation. He and I had always run in different groups – his being the popular one and mine being the not-so-popular one. After sixth grade, we'd gone off to different junior high and high schools and then colleges that were states apart.

"Audrey! How the hell are you?" He asked, pulling me into a hug.

"Me? How are you?!" I matched his enthusiasm. "I haven't seen you in years!"

Not going to lie, at this point, I expected him to become bored with me and throw out some form of the brush off, but he kept asking me questions, even flirting a little, and I was so in shock. He'd never paid this much attention to me ever, other than to let me know when one of the most embarrassing moments of my life was about to happen. We talked long enough for my best friend to wonder where I was, eventually working her way through the crowded bar to find me deep in conversation with an unexpected person. She said a quick but warm hello to him and pulled my elbow, her signal that she needed me on the other side of the bar.

CHAPTER 6: MODERN DATING AND SPECIAL-ORDER FIANCÉS

"Hey, it was great to see you, I'm really glad you're doing so well," I opted for the polite exit.

"Hey, yeah you, too. Are you free tomorrow?" I ignored her tug, my feet frozen in place.

"We should get coffee or something. What's your number?" The sixth grade king had turned into a gentleman of the nicest kind, and he wanted to have coffee with me. I passed him my number and that night, we made plans for the next day.

Let me be clear about this – when I go home for Christmas, it's strictly family time. All of my friends know this about me because it drives them crazy that I only make plans to hang out outside of my family's dinner-and-a-movie time. The fact that I was willingly giving up a precious Saturday morning to have coffee with a boy who once gave me the worst news of my life was a big deal.

The next morning, I asked my mom if I could borrow her car to meet Parker. I played it off like I was meeting up with an old friend for some much needed quality time. Even as I was backing out of the garage, I gave myself a reality check: was I really on my way to meet this guy for coffee at 9 am on the only Saturday of my Christmas break? Yes. Yes I was.

Parker smiled as he sat in the metal high top barstool across from me, and we talked together for the next couple hours. It became evident that neither one of us was interested romantically in the other person, which allowed for unfiltered conversation about life and all that we'd made of it thus far. We parted ways, having enjoyed one another's company, and I'm thankful for that moment. I'm thankful I wasn't concerned with what I was getting out of my time with him, only that we were getting time. Time to catch up, to laugh, to talk like the social beings we all need to be.

I think there is something to be said for the way that we communicate with each other when there's a subconscious desire to gain affirmation from the other person's opinion about us or their level of romantic interest. I may have been amazed at Parker's choice to call me out of the crowd that night in December, but I know that whatever potential affirmations he had to say to me or about me could be found anywhere – I didn't go into this situation looking for validation. And even though I've never had all the answers, I know that we will find what we go looking for, so we have to ask ourselves, what is it that we're looking for?

There is a moment that I've lived many times over – the moment where I decide if I'm going to believe the truth about myself that is foundational and everlasting, or the false truth I can feed into by skimming the surface of emotionally fed spaces. Sometimes, I pick the right truth, and sometimes, I pick the one that leaves me full for just a moment, and then emptier than I was before I believed it. In reconnecting with the sixth grade king, I was able to find freedom in a friendship that could have potentially been stolen if I had gone looking for his validation of my worthiness.

And that can be the danger of dating apps. We begin with good intentions of finding love, but intentions get muddled in the testing of our vanity and our ability to seek love apart from self-worth. I've deleted multiple apps before while feeling and acknowledging the loss of admiration from others; thankfully, the recognition that this kind of loss was okay, healthy even, always stood firm. Granted, this style of dating has been hugely successful for people and that makes me so happy. Having worked in the bridal industry, I've heard several stories of success from brides who have met their significant others through swiping, which makes me think that their love is the strongest kind - to swim in a sea of possibilities and choose just one for the rest of your life grows a strong love.

With growing access to online dating, that means that we have the ability to see every single one of our options before deciding on one. That is, if we can decide. While good things have come from this, I believe that the growing epidemic with my generation and younger is that with immediate access to every possible option, the ability to say "yes" to one gets harder. And then when that yes is finally said, the ability to stay committed to that one grows even more challenging.

Our current culture is so much about, "look, but don't touch." We want to swipe based upon looks and a few cheesy lines, but then when it comes to true human connection, we're severely lacking. And then our timing with the "touch" part of things comes way ahead of healthy intimacy, so intentions get murky and strong connections get made without any intention of follow-through; this is how hearts get obliterated. I call it the 30-second fallout. You swipe, you match, you start a conversation. The pressure is on to lead with some kind of witty remark that leaves you dangling over the Grand Canyon on a tightrope. Sometimes he takes the bait, sometimes he doesn't, but you're left trying to make the most of a conversation in which you can't even hear anyone's tone of voice. And heaven-forbid they don't have pictures that accurately portray all 51 of their hobbies while capturing their most photogenic side. Sheesh. Dating apps were created out of the good intention to make dating easier for people, I'm sure. But if we're not careful, the most that it does is water down our intentionality and leave us wondering why, after all that, they didn't want to meet up.

7

Chapter 7: Truth

Have you ever tasted the sour effort of striving? Have you ever pushed yourself so hard only to slump over exhausted at the finished line, confused and alone and still searching? In dating, there are many different things that encourage us to strive for an end result we think we want because we've dressed up longing and made it look like hope, or we've believed hurried lies that push us to desperation parading as a reasonable desire to love and be loved. But freedom does not come from striving, and love in its most beautiful form - the kind of love we're all hoping for and all worthy of - does not come from striving, no matter how hard we work for it or how badly we want it.

When I was in high school, I over-extended myself. I was involved in more things than what I had time for and I believed the lie that striving was going to get me where I wanted to go and keep me filled up along the way. I now know that my striving was fueled by my desire for perfection, so let's break that down for a second.

What I've finally established is that "perfection" is a unicorn word - it doesn't exist. We let culture reel us into the belief that there is a certain aesthetic or standard to be reached and if we don't measure onto that spectrum of aesthetic, we're less worthy of love and belonging. If we strive for that aesthetic, we, as women, buy more makeup, shop more, and spend money on things that promise to help us get there, and as men, vulnerability plummets to invisible depths as the bar for what it means to be masculine is set by an industry that photoshops and over-sexualizes. Thankfully, companies are starting to break that toxic mold and let originality seep in, but as a culture, it's a slow fight to get back into a healthy place once we realized how far we've already fallen.

I let my striving for perfection lead me into depression, hateful comparison, and worst of all, into the constant battle with truth that I was not enough as I was. If you had asked, I would have told you that I didn't need the compliments and admiration of others; that I was fine on my own word and knowledge. But inside, I would beg to know if you thought I was pretty, funny, talented, and enough. It was only when I would run back to God's gospel truth about me that I would finally find rest and restoration. To this day, when God reminds me of my true identity and I listen, I don't need another person's validation to be confident in my worthiness.

The trouble I got myself into in high school started here - in the battle for perfection. I misunderstood God's love for me to mean that only if I did all the right things and never said or did the wrong things that I was worthy. In short, I believed that I belonged the most when I was "getting it right." The society I grew up in furthered this backwards idea by applauding my success, my "rights," and labeling my failures as "wrongs". All of this was going on while the truth was right there in my face, but I wasn't allowing myself to step into that freedom, grabbing and consuming the truth like homemade lemonade on a hot day.

I liked the way my persona of perfection had an affect on the people I came into contact with. I liked the way they looked at me like I was a shiny token of good works and good grades, untarnished and special.

Since I let my view of doing the "right" things skew my perspective entirely, I fell into the belief that life would only be good if I did things the way they were "supposed" to be done. This included graduating high school, going to college, getting good grades, getting married, having kids, etc; I believed the lie that anything out of this order wasn't good enough. I now know that if I had seen clearly sooner, I would have done things a lot differently. But my wake up call came the night that the relationship I thought I'd been waiting for my whole life exploded in my face like a nuclear bomb.

I took pride in the idea that we'd done everything the way I always dreamt it would go, drawing boxes around different aspects of our relationship until everything fit perfectly inside. We got engaged and set a date. As the date approached, things got rocky. I suddenly became aware of the fact that I was looking around our obstacles and not really dealing with them. I was pretending that everything would be alright instead of acknowledging the actual size of the conflicts - like icebergs floating in chilly blue water they bobbed, exposing only the very tip of something monstrous and unknown. I kept pushing. I thought that if we just stuck to the plan that looked good on paper, we would make it though. Just keep pushing, Audrey, keep striving. I wanted to be right and couldn't bear to admit defeat. My white flag of surrender would never be waved. I called it loyalty, but really it was pride that kept me from admitting the truth that everyone else saw: we were a sinking ship that desperately needed its life boats inflated for the call to abandon ship.

The night he ended it, my life fell apart. My glass haven of pretend perfection was shattered. I was suddenly an unwilling passenger on a rollercoaster of shock, anger, and utter disbelief. I'd never truly understood betrayal before, but here I was, betrayal's prisoner, unable to see my way out of its cell. I was unexpectedly faced with the best decision of my life: am I who this massive disappointment is telling me I am, or am I who my Creator says I am?

Rejection. Psychologically speaking, rejection triggers pathways in the brain that are also used to register physical pain. We *physically* feel rejection, not just emotionally. Just as I have personally been rejected by other people in my life, my strive for perfection was rejected in an earth-shattering ground-splitting way that caused a physical disruption in my beliefs and in the way I lived my life that night.

I started rebuilding my life from ground zero, picking up pieces of rubble and piling them where I thought they should go. One pile for truth, one for lies, one for the past that was hopeless to salvage. This wasn't like the rejection I felt when I learned that my crush had asked out another girl at the base of the snowboard hill in fifth grade. This required the daily recognition that my worth was not and would never be dependent upon another person's thoughts, opinion, or approval of me. Even though he didn't choose me, nothing about my worthiness changed. Eventually, this daily reminder grew into the steady knowledge that my worth is an unwavering stake in the ground; it is not up for debate or questioning. It is not looking to be proved.

My identity as being worthy of love and worth loving is an undeniable fact that I don't need to look to others for affirmation of, once and for all. If I had decided on anything else, to this day, I would still be trying to fill that question with a million other things, from people to addictions to repetitive behaviors that would leave me feeling more unsure about myself and so unlovable. I know this to be true because in those moments that I doubt my worth, I have a choice of what I turn to for a reminder of truth. I've chosen the things that parade as those reminders, but there is nothing like the sweet relief of stepping back into the ultimate truth of my worth that is found only in who God says I am.

Having my heart broken and world smashed was, looking back, the grandest thing that could have happened to me at 25. I got my chance at a do-over, and I finally started to understand the truth that God's love was not at all simultaneous with me getting things "right," but instead had everything to do with me saying yes to receiving His grace; grace that filled the gaps of whatever kind of cracking or breaking I could ever experience in this life. It's not the flawlessly smooth surface of life we should be proud of, but all of the cracks in our history that, like moments of honesty, let the light shine through.

As cheesy as it may be, the song that got me through this time was *Don't Be So Hard On Yourself* by Jess Glynn. It reminded me that I'd been chasing something that wasn't real and I needed to give myself a break. I needed to return to living in freedom and truth, because God's perfect love for me casts out all fear. The only thing that would ever be perfect in my life was the way God loved me and continues to love me to this day — it's His fully formed and unchanging acceptance I need to rest in and His opinion of me that matters, and He has a pretty high one.

8

Chapter 8: Inner Revelation

"Watch over your heart with all diligence, for from it flows the spring of life."
Proverbs 4:23

We have to be willing to open ourselves up to the process of self-evaluation. Our motives, postures, egos, and actions all have a reason for being, so what is that reason? Or maybe there's more than one reason. We must always ask ourselves "why".

Self-evaluation calls on humility; it is not a need to be right, it is the need to participate that shows respect to your relationships, your friendships, and to yourself. Participation that invites the elimination of selfish desires and replaces them with a desire for greater good. It's not a loss of freedom, but a holy invitation to bring your truest and most honest self to the surface and see what arises. It's like unclogging a drain that for years has been fed clumps of lies and translucency, suffocating the potential for a full and steady stream of truth to pass through.

Emotions are so powerfully felt that they can sometimes feel like everything. But emotions are also the first things to make us selfish; we want something to go a certain way or be a certain thing purely because of how we *feel* about it. Watching over your heart is not making sure you get everything you want or everything you think you're deserving of, it's posturing yourself so that if you need to re-evaluate your priorities and renew your thoughts, you have the capacity to do so free of emotional attachment. On the flip side, it's also not nailing up boards and setting up iron bars for protection from vulnerability, either. It's putting in the necessary everyday work to make sure our heart is in line with the Father's heart. His heart is peace, unity, good news, sacrifice, come as you are, rest here, renewal, light, resurrection, and hope. He calls us out of the darkness of self-indulgence and a too-tight emotional grip and into the light. The light unearths, reveals, restores and is one hundred percent necessary for growth. The tricky part here is to be able to identify if your motives are fear-based or freedom-based.

We can guard our hearts for what feels like protection while really just being afraid to trust in the Father's goodness - that what He has for us is truly meant for our prosperity. And not a worldly prosperity, but one that exceeds what we can even imagine. We have to be willing to lay it all on the line to see what He says about it. Our fears are fully tested against His heart for us and over time, as we let Him show us His true nature, we discover that those fears aren't worth holding on to anymore. We can let go of every fear and find complete peace in His arms. *Let me just say real quick that I use the pronoun He/His for God because that is relatable to our culture. Do I put God into a masculine box in my own personal life? Absolutely not. For more on this, I recommend reading *Wearing God: Clothing, Laughter, Fire, and Other Overlooked Ways of Meeting God* by Lauren F. Winner.

If we carry fear into our relationships, it weighs heavily on those we love. If we let fear or worry scare us back into our comfortable corner of control, we never work through the reasons why we are afraid in the first place and the wholeness of life becomes difficult to experience. We all

CHAPTER 8: INNER REVELATION

have reasons to be afraid; past hurts, losses, emotional trauma, betrayal, physical pain, loneliness, abandonment - the list could go on forever. But equally long and forever cancelling-out are the reasons we have to not let those fears have the final say over our decisions. I once heard a pastor pose the question, "are you experiencing suffering, or are you just uncomfortable?"

 It took me two years to work through the pain of that break up. It was an engagement and with that, I had made endless plans for our future together and the life that we wanted to make. There were so many steps to the process of restoration and I knew in my heart of hearts that if I didn't take them all, I would live lugging around a heavy burden on my shoulders, never able to fully trust or love someone again. For me, this process began with grieving the loss of someone I had believed to be my best friend and my person, in my corner and on my side. I loved him, and now I had to feel what it felt like to let love die slowly from one ten-minute conversation. I had to find closure on my own by walking through the stages of heartbreak, which looked something like anger, denial, loss, frustration, hopelessness, and eventually, forgiveness. I finally grasped the reality behind certain verses in scripture, like Psalm 34:18: "The Lord **is near to the brokenhearted** and saves the crushed in spirit." I leaned hard into my friends and let them love me without feeling like I owed them anything back. Arriving at the conclusion that I was the only person responsible for my capacity to heal, I took what was my last step in the process of healing from heartbreak: forgiveness. Ultimately, I believed there was freedom waiting for me in the letting go, and so I did just that.

 As I let go of the hurt, I walked into new life and redemption that let me press into God's promises and his loving-kindness. I re-learned that the level to which I belonged was not determined by another person's opinion. I renewed my belief in the truth of my worthiness. I let it come up in conversation and let others talk me through my emotions, never pretending to be a certain way because I didn't want to feel it. I came as I was.

I did the work required for restoration. Just like unforeseen earthquakes raze cities, intentional work builds them back up. The last piece to this puzzle was forgiving everyone I felt had hurt me during the breakup process and truly giving thanks for everyone in my life who had risen to the occasion of my heartbreak. I took the time to say out loud who I needed to forgive and why, with the full knowledge that they may never come to ask for that forgiveness. Verbalizing forgiveness allowed me to practice the same grace that I knew had been poured out over me. I took responsibility for anything I needed to and without letting that bring self-deprecation, I moved on in the full knowledge of the fact that I was loved unconditionally by my Father and I could plant my roots by His life-giving water for rest. He wrote me love letters and I finally took them to heart:

My love is not like theirs;
My love is unwavering. It doesn't come and go.
I don't need to experience more of you to love you more - I love you just as you are.
I love you wholeheartedly right in this immediate moment.
My love cannot be taken away, and it chases you down when you try to run from it.
My love does not hinge on how well you perform.
My love has nothing to do with what I can get from you, and everything to do with what I have given to you and will continue to give you all the days of your life.

The truth hurts, but the truth also brings freedom, and the truth is that we've all done things we wish we hadn't. We've all succumbed to our human nature in ways that require forgiveness. Realizing that we need forgiveness for things just as much as we need to forgive other people for things that they've done to us is our baseline where true healing comes from. Sometimes, we have to forgive people without them knowing. Sometimes, we have to ask them for forgiveness face to face or give them the opportunity to forgive us face to face. This is hard for so many reasons, but mainly because it invites us into vulnerability and humility on every level. But like we've already talked about, vulnerable people are the ones that have the most joy in their lives. In short, forgiveness = joy.

We've all met people that are harboring some kind of offense committed against them - they walk with bitter steps, trudging along carrying this "unforgiveness" like a rain cloud; heavy laden with sour moods and sensitivity. Maybe, this cloud has even grown into hatred and anger, and the weight is like painful daggers pressing against their heart every time this person has a social experience. It's easy for us to look as this person and call out what they're carrying - it's harder for us to look at our own lives and see the same struggle. But if we don't, our relationships suffer and the people around us end up bearing the consequences of our rain cloud.

If I haven't emphasized this enough already, forgiveness sets us free. So, who do you need to forgive? From whom do you need to ask for forgiveness?

Forgiveness allows us to experience joy unlaced with the sour taste of past faults. It allows us to sip sweetly from the relational depths we're offered in this life. When we cling to our hurts and ignore the option of forgiveness, we carry bitterness around like a battered travel pack, constantly setting up camp in our brokenness.

Those people you need to ask for forgiveness from and those who need to forgive you: you deserve to be free from these things. You were made to walk uprightly into your future, not while being weighed down by everything that's happened to you and everything you've done that you wish you hadn't. Maybe the person that needs the most forgiveness is yourself.

9

Chapter 9: Tell It Like It Is and More Forgiveness

What I've come to realize about dating is that there's no formula. There's no "right way" or checklist provided to make sure we don't screw it up - we are going to screw it up and that's the whole point; learning from our mistakes and being willing to apologize first; not being afraid to look like a fool because we need to ask for something; laying down our pride to treat the other person with honor and the full knowledge of their true worth; maintaining self-accountability so that we stay honest and kind. Our power comes in the recognition that God is always working, so we get to choose to release whatever brokenness we are carrying around or causing ourselves - we can choose to deny His presence or we can choose to let it change us and guide us.

Combined, my early ideas about men, my desire to do things "the right way," and my longing to avoid vulnerability led me to all of my relationships until I was 28. Oh, let's not forget the ache to be affirmed and admired. During all of those dating escapades, I kept a close relationship with God; just close enough so that I could keep my eye on Him and keep peace with His holy spirit. But He was less concerned with my preference and more concerned with the fact that I was willing to sell myself short to make relationships work. He was more concerned with the fact that I thought I had to be perfect or do it right, and He proved that by pulling me close every time a relationship ended and reminding me that I was cherished, known, and loved, and belonged to Him regardless of what the shambles of the last relationship were telling me. I could stand on my own as a single woman and regurgitate these lovely thoughts, but that's not when I really needed them the most. It was in those hard spaces of loss that I learned truth was not to be taken lightly and was meant for every moment, not just when I felt like choosing it.

God cares way more about us laying down our striving and resting with Him in a place of openness - He wants us to abide in His presence so that we carry the full assurance of our worth no matter where we go or what happens or who we meet. He wants to be right there with us, whispering over our shoulder that we are His and we don't have to prove how worthy we are to anyone else. We just get to be ourselves. Why is it, by the way, that as we become adults, we have to re-learn that? We're always telling kids to "just be themselves," but we rarely take our own advice. I once heard this described as, "reconciling your flesh to your spirit."

In December of 2015 when I said "yes" to a real marriage proposal, it was my third marriage proposal, the first being in first grade under that large Oak Tree, the second being in response to a comment I made once in a man's fishing boat:

Jeremy: "Gosh I'm sorry, there's no room on my boat, there are too many fishing poles."

Audrey: "No such thing."

Jeremy pauses, looks up with a fishing pole in each hand and says, "marry me?"

15-year-old Audrey who has a MASSIVE crush on the much older

CHAPTER 9: TELL IT LIKE IT IS AND MORE FORGIVENESS

Jeremy: "...yes."

But back to the real proposal. We met at a wedding and dated for a year and change. I'm not going to make any comments on the relationship itself that I haven't already made, but I will take full responsibility for my desire to have done it 'perfectly'. Here were my boxes:

Make sure he was a christian

No sex before marriage

Date intentionally

Have a great relationship with his family

Stay together at all costs, yada yada

When you take these out of context, they don't seem like bad things. But for me, I wrapped them in a heavy wet towel monogrammed with the initials of massively unhealthy striving for perfection, M.U.S.P, and now I'm here to tell you to let it go. Stop being so hard on yourself. Build yourself up in love from the purest source and know that when you mess things up, there's so much grace for you. Be a purveyor of grace for others when they mess things up. This is the reason why we need to be aware of our expectations that we have for ourselves and for others. This is why we need to let them go and re-define them through a lens of grace. My mom actually wore those glasses in the 80s, I think, the massive ones that nearly covered her whole face because they were so big. Put those glasses on and let the lenses be thick - layer after layer of healing, forgiving, rest-inspiring grace.

I still approach potential relationships with similar hopes. I would love for my future spouse to know God and share in glorifying Him with me through our relationship. But that looks a lot less like getting things right and a lot more like being willing to apply grace to every situation no matter what happens. I would love to stay faithful to my future husband by reserving sex for my marriage, but not because I want to be perfect. Instead, I want to honor the design in which I want to experience intimacy. Now, it has nothing to do with a desire to "be right" or "get it right" like it used to. I would love to have an amazing relationship with my future spouse's family. But you know what, you can't win 'em all and even if I don't ride the same wave as someone else, I can still love them and let grace fill the gaps of our differences.

This might sound crazy, but now I have the ability to be thankful for God's movement through my relationships. What I mean is, I would let God end every relationship I've ever had time and time again if it meant that through that, I had the opportunity to know and learn the depth of His love for me. He cares light years more about my capacity for knowing Him and loving Him and understanding my worth because of His love for me than He does about me being in a relationship. And when the time is truly right - whatever that looks like - it will happen.

In the meantime, we get to fall into His lake of grace. I picture it like this:

Lemonade on a lake in the summer and the mounting excitement towards the thrill of running and jumping off the end of the dock over and over again. And then one summer day, you're running and you hear bare feet skimming the wooden dock in the space next to you, and you look over at that person, who looks back at you with a grin on their face, and you both jump. You grab hands and pick your feet up underneath you, ready to break the surface of that cool refreshing lake together.

10

Chapter 10: Healing

A natural expectation from our human nature is to relate to the people, ideas, and things around us; connection is one of the greatest joys of being human. We take our experiences and translate them into songs, words, and conversations in order to lift up and reach out to other people. Personally, I love this about being human. I think knowing other people's stories and sharing my own is one of the most beautiful things about being alive. I believe that the more transparent and upfront we are about our experiences, the more we get out of life. The danger here is that we mislead each other into believing that because we had an experience go a certain way, theirs will go the same way. Because we are emotional beings, it's easy to let our emotions dictate how we perceive and re-tell experiences. Even if we're living our life from a place of foundational truth, we can easily let our experiences turn into mistranslated emotional information for another person.

Connection is beautiful when it's used in a way to uplift and encourage, but if we fixate on the lyrics in a song or the words strung together in a romantic poem to the point that they become emotional direction, we're not feeding our deepest sense of truth. Don't get me wrong, these are not bad things, but if we're using them as our point of direction, then we're walking ourselves right off the deep end of our feelings. We have to be able to sort truth from how we feel and fight the urge to feed our feelings with what we think we want - because the reality is, we're creatures of habit who fight what's good for us until it's smacking us upside the face for attention. We can still be deeply romantic without feeling like another person completes us. We can still appreciate the reality of love and commitment without feeling like we can't go on without those things in our lives. We're stronger than our emotions lead us to believe. Feelings are true and valuable, but they are not the *ultimate* truth. So, the big question, where does the truth lie? Is it hidden away in books? Layered in the distraction of movies? We can feel it there, but we can only know it from one source.

The forgotten foundation of life is that we are beings designed for intimacy - ultimately, intimacy with our creator. But the world shows us hundreds of different places where we can derive shallow intimacy, and so we keep falling for it. The world is also quick to tell us that we aren't worthy of true intimacy or that because we're weird or different or because we've messed up, we don't deserve it. But we have to realize that abundant life will never be found in these things - these things that falsely promise to complete us and make us happy. It's that classic case of fixating on the things we think will make life better, only to finally get them and realize that we still want more.

Intimacy was not intended to be short handed; to be lit up and tossed aside like an expended firework. It was meant to be explored in ways that draw us closer to the truth about who we are. Intimacy was meant to be explored in a way that grows our ability to experience vulnerability, peeling back our layers of fear, mistrust, and lies.

In our culture, we hear intimacy and immediately think sex, but that's not it. Sex is definitely part of it, but we're missing 90% of intimacy when we just think of it physically.

When I was 19, I shared my first kiss with my first boyfriend. It was the night after a Halloween party at the baseball house off campus. Slowly, we inched towards each other and the ends of our individual pillows until there was no place left to go but lip lock city. Before him, there was only ever one other guy that I'd wanted to kiss, and that never played out. Probably for good reason.

Up until the night of the kiss, we had been spending casual time together. Something about being around him kept me quiet, a red flag that you're probably not supposed to be with that person, I now realize. But let me just say, this had little to do with him, and everything to do with my desire for him to find me attractive and to keep me around, regardless of how I was treated. I was afraid that if I opened my mouth, I'd say something he wouldn't like and he would never want to see me again. I held back from showing him my true self because I didn't want it to be so rejected. Speechlessness: a fine quality in a future wife, hands down.

I'm kidding, you guys. I think as women, we do face the challenge of being pursued more than men tend to be pursued, and yes, I said challenge. This subconscious storyline tells us to wait for the man and to not act out of turn according to society's past courtship requirements. We're still recovering from the era of "keep your opinions to yourself and have dinner ready by six" that was generations before us. I know that we don't all suffer from this, but I definitely believe that part of the reason I never fully spoke up with my first romantic interest was because of the fear that if I did, he wouldn't validate me and I'd be discarded. But let's squash that lie - as women, we DO NOT need to be validated. We need to be heard, respected, held accountable to truth, and loved by those we are in relationship with, but the belief that we need another's opinion of or connection to us to validate our worth is utter bullshit that, given the opportunity, will crush our spirit into silence, desperation, and anxiety. Without our true worth, we're left hanging onto a thread of shallow affirmation disguised as hope that, when it breaks, leaves us jumping from relationship to relationship seeking shelter.

Also tied to this mentality is our old friend, fear. Notice how I mentioned that "I was afraid that..." The way I see it, fear is either a liar determined to hold you back, or a bell tolling reckoning for you and the fact that death is inevitable – because the most final end result of any situation is always death. But even death can't win because if anything, it holds us all together; it's the one thing we all have in common. It's what we do with the middle section between birth and death that matters, and fear is the thing that either keeps us quiet with our heads down or brings us to loud irrational anger. Fear does not lead us to freedom or intentionality, but instead holds us back in our pursuit of the vulnerable and thus the pursuit of true joy. I intend to enjoy every second of my middle section, so fear can go shut itself in my sixth grade locker.

And men, pursuing a woman requires courage and self-control. It takes time and some restraint – before you kiss her, you need to learn three things: her middle name, her favorite color, and what she believes in. If you don't know these, wait. I promise you, it will be WAY better the more you know about her. Also, you don't fly through these questions to get there. Let them come up organically; actually LEARN them.

If you think about kissing as purely physical, it's not hard to come by. Been there, done that. But if you think about it as something meant to be shared with a person you want to pursue, it's different. Some people wait to kiss until their wedding day, and you thought date number two was hard.

What God had shown me about my worth before I started dating my first boyfriend is that my true worth would never be derived from any amount of physical intimacy I would experience or from words of flattery. Because of this truth, I decided that I would never go "all the way" with someone until we were married. This set the precedent for me in a way I'm still thankful for today. I believe that it is one million times harder to heal from a relationship where physical boundaries were broken, and

CHAPTER 10: HEALING

I think that if you've been there like me, you'll agree. God showed me that true intimacy is meant to be a picture of me alone with Him, being honest about my hopes, dreams, and fears, and being fully known, so that I can extend the way that I know Him in the form of a loving hand outstretched to friends and others. He did design us for intimacy - first with Him, then with each other. He has so much to say to us about who we are and what we mean to Him, and we miss the most important part of our story if we skip His prequel and jump right into our own novel.

Unfortunately, I didn't keep to the mindset of waiting to be married before taking steps into physical intimacy. The idea of sex is so alluring, and while there's nothing creative about temptation, we still fall for it. I've tried to think of ways that I could break the spell of having sex in a way that other women decide not to be coerced by it. There are so many things that encourage us towards sex - loving a person, physical pleasure, feeling wanted, and the lie that if we don't do it, we're missing out.

I love what Corinthians 7 says about this. The writer, Paul, doesn't pretend like people don't want to have sex. Don't get it twisted - I'm not at all saying that the purpose of marriage is just to have sex. But Paul writes in verse 2:

"Since sexual immorality is occurring, each man should have sexual relations with his own wife, and each wife with her own husband." Paul gets it. He knows that people want to have sex - God designed pleasure after all, and like getting ice cream or listening to a mixed cd from your person, it's meant to be connective and intimate. *So* connecting and *so* intimate in fact, that He gives it a special place: with your husband or with your wife. He takes that night at the carnival and says, "all that and more." But we have a tendency to mess that up. As we get older, we let the little things lose their luster and think the bigger things will bring us what we want. But done out of context, they leave us worse than they found us.

Ultimately, all that I can say is that it's just not worth it. I have found that in those moments that I feel weak in the knees over believing the lie that I'm missing out on sex, I make a choice that is not at all rooted in the truth of my worthiness. It's not at all an issue of condemnation like so many cultures are quick to force on us, it's an issue of acknowledging the wounds that remind us that we are unworthy, unwanted, and unloved so that we can stand in the face of those lies and pull them up by the roots to replace them with the truth of how loved, wanted, and worthy we are without needing to invite the superficial feelings of these things through a physical act of pleasure. Healing from these moments is not an easy thing and healing from relationships that tore through the boundaries of physical intimacy can be gut wrenching. This piece of connection designed to be the ultimate display of intimacy entangles us in unhealthy places when done for the sake of experience.

How do we get to the point of breakthrough when everything in our life is distracting us into different directions? We literally have to hold still. Put your feet firmly on the floor. Close your eyes, and take the deepest breath you've ever taken. Exhale for six seconds. When you open your eyes, think of the most important thing in your life. Write it down. Is that where the majority of your energy is going? Or are your thoughts being distracted by worry, derailed by busyness, thrown off by fantasy?

I once heard a pastor say that "vision without action is fantasy." And if you're letting the daydreams of what you want sway your emotions, you've lost twice - daydreaming steals your ability to make your vision for your life a reality because it keeps you preoccupied *while* continuing to bring you emotionally back to a place of fantasy. You keep living in your dream world because it feels better to go there than to face reality. But taking that first step out of fantasy and into your actual vision is hard because now you have something to lose — something to be held accountable to. This is vulnerable and this is hard, but it is worth every single painful step.

CHAPTER 10: HEALING

There seemed to be two ends of this spectrum in my life that I would swing back and forth between. I would either live in a make-believe world where my crush took on certain qualities because I would burden him with expectations before getting to know him, or I would think that my validation hinged on my crush having mutual affection for me. When all of this came to light, I realized that I needed to re-sort out my life's priorities and find breakthrough, because another person's validation was not going to give me any more worth than what I already had.

At that same moment, I was given the chance to put into practice healthy boundaries and the chance to honor my crush by standing by my word as a friend, so that they felt safe and respected. Speaking out emotions gives you the power and authority over them *before* you act on them. If you need distance from this person, you have the opportunity to be honest about that, too, which is also worth it. You've just done a mature and courageous act by saying, "this is how I feel and I'm taking ownership of it by honoring you with the truth." You've practiced vulnerability. (I say practice because let's be honest, not a single one of us will ever be any good at it.) The catch? It has to be done and said in a matter free from expectation.

Remember that part about me needing to tell my crushes how I feel? This directly applies to that. And speaking of my *Liar Liar* tongue, I have an embarrassing story for you, but there's a victory for vulnerability at the end, I promise.

In my mid-twenties, I developed a crush on a guy who also happened to be one of my neighbors. Ironically, before this happened, I made a personal pact to never catch feelings for someone who lived in my same apartment complex; a defense mechanism aimed toward keeping things "neat and tidy," I suppose. Well, the truth is that we can't help who we have feelings for, but we can help what we do with them. I barely knew this guy, but I knew I wanted him to like me (who can relate?). Over the course of a few weeks, I received a myriad of mixed signals from him and all throughout, I tried to keep my cool. One night, I went out with a couple girlfriends to have a low-key GNO, only to be surprised by my crush's request to join us. I assumed his inviting himself was evidence that he wanted to spend time with me so badly, that he was willing to suffer through girls' night to make it happen. What they say about assumption rings true.

We all arrived at our first stop of the night only to be met with the surprise that a few other friends were there and also that as we traversed on to our initial end point for the evening, he wanted to stay with those other friends instead of accompanying us onward. Well, jealousy took hold in my soul and I needed little persuasion that the rest of the evening's intention was reserved for making him jealous.

As we entered my most beloved dive bar and favorite dancing spot (they play retired episodes of Soul Train on their TVs, how could you not love it here), we ran into friends that one of us hadn't seen in a long time. I quickly noticed how attractive one of these new faces was and casually joined into the game they were all playing, so that I could toss him side-glances and flirty hints. It worked, and the second my crush walked into the bar to meet us, I was dancing karaoke style to AC/DC with my new-found male interest. Friends looking on reported a response of shock and awe from the guy I claimed to have feelings for and labeled the night a success.

Looking back, I would never try to excuse my motives by saying it was just flirting - I have pretty strict boundaries for myself and I know what happens once you start toeing that line. But, I still felt horrible. We ended up giving the new guy a ride home at the end of the night, prequel-ed by a small but noticeable "my horse is bigger than your horse" quarrel as I sat between the two of them in the backseat. A guilty rose between two thorns.

The next day, I was brimming with conviction - I was never one to use shady motives to bring someone into my life, and I couldn't handle the

CHAPTER 10: HEALING

thought that this person whose friendship I said I valued became a target of my prickly jealousy. I let my thoughts brine in a stew of indecision over the next few days and ultimately decided that this was not how I would've wanted to be treated; I would've wanted my friend to be open and honest with me about how they were feeling and trust me with their vulnerability. To me, that's a sign of respect and courage — a true sign of feelings that extends beyond games and shallow emotional responses. Honesty reaches out past selfishness and treats the other person with honor.

I texted him to let him know that I had something I wanted to talk to him about. My fingers left a little print of sweat on my phone with every touch. I hated the build-up, but I knew the release would be worth it. The next thing I had to think about was being honest with him about how I felt without making him feel like he owed me anything for it. I didn't want him to feel like my emotions were his responsibility and I knew that I had to be honest without expectation, mostly including his response - a response I had no control over. I think I blacked out while walking over to his place.

My heart-to-heart with him included an apology for treating him like less than he was worth by using someone else to make him jealous. I felt like a scummy person for doing that to him, and no one should ever be made to feel that way, regardless of previous circumstances.

I was going to tell you how he responded, but then I realized, that's not the important part. The important part is holding ourselves accountable to a standard that treats ourselves and each other with abounding grace free from manipulation and selfishness, just like Jesus would and did. When our actions allow freedom to flourish, people see the heart of God; they see how worthy of love they are. We may not get it all right the first time, or second, or third, but know that there is always an opportunity to offer the world what you have been offered yourself. And it's grace that helps us get there.

The bottom line is that we're going to hurt one another – that's inevitable. In all kinds of relationships, it's people from different backgrounds, mindsets, and systems of belief coming together, trying to communicate effectively and enjoy one another's company. Forgiveness lets us take our relationships with others to an amazing place because it makes pride's seat at the table disappear the second we decide to actually choose to forgive or to ask for forgiveness. It's admitting that we know we are not perfect, paving the way for humility and a greater understanding of who we truly and beautifully are. It's knowing that forgiveness heals, no matter how long after the offense you decide to use it. In my mind, forgiveness is the greatest example of love. Love without forgiveness is an unrealistic storyline. Grace is always close when forgiveness is present, and it's grace that we need the most. Grace while we're fumbling over the words to say, searching for the best ones. Grace when the day has been long and hard, but you have a phone call scheduled with your person because one of you is out of town. Grace when everything you thought you wanted disappears, and you rebuild your life with even stronger priorities. Grace to try it again with more clarity, more vulnerability, and more joy.

11

Chapter 11: The End

I used to think that none of this would make sense or have any validity unless I was married by the time this book made its way out into the world - old habits die hard, I guess. I felt like I wanted to prove that everything in these pages could be tested by evidence; proof that marriage is found at the end of it all. But then I realized that marriage is not a byproduct of any formula and we don't get to learn our worthiness or who God truly is because something we've always wanted has come to fruition. We learn who God is in the throes of the process of getting to know Him, therefore knowing ourselves. And if this journey doesn't fit into our idea of dating, that's when we know we're going about it all backwards.

I said it earlier and it's still true: I would be at peace with God if He brought every relationship I had to an end if it meant that I was given the opportunity to draw closer to Him and learn more about His character and unending, unwavering love for me. Another person will never be able to meet our needs because our Creator does that first. Another person is simply a gift - a beautiful soul we are blessed with who compliments our nature and spurs us on in the pursuit of truth, reminding us of how loved we already are, and how incredibly cool is it that we get to do the same for them. This is why it is so important that we grow. We get to practice these things in friendship all our lives; walking through forgiveness, healing, intentionality, and at the core of it all, vulnerability. After all, if my friends aren't the ones standing up next to me in support of my marriage because they can bear witness to the kind of friend and wife I'm capable of being, I don't want to be married at all.

We have to be willing to give ourselves space to wrestle with these things. If we avoid them, we end up bringing them into our relationships and beyond. Some marriages are strong enough to handle this unearthing and rewiring, some are not. It's okay to be a work in progress - honestly, I think I'll be a work in progress my entire life. But I have finally come to the place where I can own that. I can say that I've explored the depths of past hurts, past relationships, and everything in between. There is no greater moment of arrival than realizing what you've been through no longer defines you, but grants you the freedom to move forward into a life of wholeness with grace as your forever guide, leading you along a map marked with forgiveness. I'm here for your journey and I'm so grateful that you've been here through mine.

Made in the USA
Coppell, TX
02 March 2021